Ida M. Tarbell

Pioneer Woman
Journalist and Biographer

by Adrian A. Paradis

CHILDRENS PRESS ®

CHICAGO

PICTURE ACKNOWLEDGMENTS

Drake Well Museum—2, 8, 20, 26, 62, 63, 66, 104
The Bettmann Archive—54, 64
Historical Pictures Service, Chicago—65 (2 photos), 67, 70, 80
Standard Oil (New Jersey) Collection, Photographic Archives,
University of Louisville—68, 69
Cover illustration by Len W. Meents

Library of Congress Cataloging in Publication Data

Paradis, Adrian A.
    Ida M. Tarbell, pioneer woman journalist and biographer.

    Includes index.
    Summary: A biography of an American author/journalist
whose exposure of dishonesty in the huge Standard Oil
Company was instrumental in its destruction as a trust,
giving small oil companies a chance to compete.
    1. Tarbell, Ida M. (Ida Minerva), 1857-1944—
Juvenile literature. 2. Journalists—United States—
Biography—Juvenile literature.
[1. Tarbell, Ida M. (Ida Minerva), 1857-1944. 2. Journalists]
I. Title. II. Series.
PN4874.T23P37   1985   070'.92'4 [B] [92]   85-16586
ISBN 0-516-03217-8

   2 3 4 5 6 7 8 9 10 R 94 93 92 91 90 89 88 87 86

Table of Contents

Ida Minerva Tarbell and her mother, Esther Ann
McCullough Tarbell, November 5, 1858

Chapter 1

A TALE OF TRUSTS

The United States enjoyed a period of prosperity after the Spanish-American War ended in 1898. Corporations were making large profits and many of them formed trusts, copying the successful organization of the Standard Oil Company of New Jersey.

The Standard Oil Company was founded in 1872 as the South Improvement Company with John D. Rockefeller at its head. Rockefeller believed competition in business was wasteful. He said that if companies joined together and formed a trust, they could eliminate waste and become very efficient. His goal was to get rid of all companies in the oil business that did not join the Standard Oil trust.

This was bad for small companies, but even worse was that Standard Oil forced railroads to carry its oil at lower rates than they charged producers and refiners who were not part of the trust. Rockefeller also persuaded the railroads to give his trust "drawbacks," or refunds, on every barrel of oil shipped by other companies. This meant that Standard Oil could charge less for its oil than did small companies (like Ida Tarbell's father's) and put most of them out of business. Then, having gotten much of the oil business for itself, Standard Oil could charge the public whatever it wished.

The old American idea that businesses should be free to compete fairly with each other seemed to be dying. Many small businessmen were discouraged because the federal Anti-Trust Law that Congress had passed in 1890 had not stopped the trusts. What, they asked, could be done now?

In 1900 the staff of *McClure's Magazine*, where Ida Tarbell worked as a journalist, discussed that and other matters. Ida recalled her father's oil tank business; how he had become a small oil producer; how he then was put out of business by Rockefeller's Standard Oil Company. She suggested writing a history of the Rockefeller company.

In the fall of 1904 Ida Tarbell's *The History of the Standard Oil Company* was published. The work exposed the unfair practices a large corporation used to gain a monopoly in its field. This led to the breakup of Standard Oil's thirty-eight companies.

The fact that a woman had written so effective an exposé in 1904 (sixteen years before women had the right to vote) astonished many people. But to those who knew Ida Tarbell and her background, it was no surprise.

Chapter 2

YOUNG WOMAN WITH A PURPOSE

Erie County, in the northwest corner of Pennsylvania, was still rough country in November, 1857, when Ida Minerva Tarbell was born in her maternal grandparents' farmhouse. The Walter McCulloughs had come as pioneers to that part of the state many years before. Their home was a story-and-a-half Cape Cod style house built of matched logs. A huge fireplace warmed the living room; there were sleeping rooms upstairs.

In the spring of the year Ida was born, her father, Franklin Sumner Tarbell, traveled alone out to Iowa. There he planned to build a home for his wife, Esther Ann, and the baby they were expecting. He had purchased land and started to construct a house when a financial panic hit the country. First, banks closed in the east and many people lost their money, then closings spread west to Iowa. Mr. Tarbell was wiped out, too, and was forced to set out for home.

Ida was a year and a half old when Mr. Tarbell returned home in 1859 to the daughter he had never seen.

"Go away, bad man!" the little girl cried as she clung to her mother. She was jealous and afraid of this stranger who now lived in their home. Her father did go away. Previously he had been not only a teacher and an expert carpenter, but also a skilled river pilot. Known as Captain Tarbell, he had been in charge of many fleets of flatboats that sailed up and down the Allegheny and Ohio rivers. By taking one last trip down the Ohio in August, 1859, he earned enough money to move the family to the farm in Iowa.

Traveling back east he heard rumors that oil had been discovered in Erie County, Pennsylvania. Rock oil had indeed been found along a stream called Oil Creek near Titusville, a small town about forty miles from the McCullough farm. Those who refined, or purified, the oil and poured it into their lamps, found that it illuminated better than the whale or coal oil then in use. Some men even said that if enough petroleum were found at Oil Creek, perhaps the whole world could be lighted by oil!

Mr. Tarbell mulled over what he had heard. He wondered where all the oil that was spouting up from the earth would be put. Then he had an idea. Why not build wooden tanks to hold the black liquid until it could be shipped to distant cities? Perhaps instead of going to Iowa, it would be wiser to move to Oil Creek and start a business making tanks.

In October of 1860 Mr. Tarbell packed the family's belongings in a wagon. He helped his wife climb up onto the front seat and handed her William, their new baby, and finally Ida. They drove forty miles over and around the mountains to Rouseville just below Titusville. The contrast between this new sprawling town and her grandparents' farm surprised and dismayed three-year-old Ida.

In the small shanty Mr. Tarbell had built for them there was a kitchen, a bedroom, and a living room. Mr. Tarbell's carpenter's shop was next to the house and soon provided the only safe place for Ida to play. Here was an ever-growing pile of soft wood shavings where she could jump, roll, play house, or take a nap.

Outside, the yard full of danger was no place for a child to play. Nearby was a high derrick. Large pools of black oil made walking difficult. Black grease covered all the trees and bushes. Here and there were piles of sand, rocks, and clay that had come from below ground; close by, water swirled and gurgled in the creek. Ida suffered endless scoldings and sometimes a switching as her mother kept warning her not to stray from home, climb the derrick rigging, or investigate pools of oil.

One day the girl told her mother, "I'm going to leave. Going back to grandmother."

"Very well," her mother said calmly, and then watched as her daughter walked away from the house. Ida continued until she came to a slight embankment that looked like a mountain to her. She stopped and decided she could go no farther. She returned home and sat wearily on the front steps. Her mother opened the door.

"Ida! You're back! I thought you had gone to grandma's."

"I don't know the way," she half whispered.

"All right, then come in and have your supper."

This was Ida's first revolt, the first time she showed a desire for independence. She was to rebel or change her plans many times during her lifetime, but whenever she decided to return home, her parents always welcomed her without questioning or harsh words.

As Ida later wrote in her memoirs, "My mother always let me carry out my revolts, return when I would and no questions asked."

When Mr. Tarbell started making oil tanks he wondered if he had made a wise decision. Business was slow and there was no money to buy extras. On that first Christmas, candy and nuts were all the parents could afford to give their children.

"Just you wait," Ida's father said, "the day will come."

The day arrived in 1861 when several new wells came in, gushing from three hundred to three thousand barrels every twenty-four hours! Now there was tremendous need for Mr. Tarbell's huge wooden tanks.

All the wells brought new danger, however. One day there was a terrible explosion. Someone had carelessly lighted a fire near an oil well, igniting some of the gas that had escaped from the earth with the oil. Flames fanned out and, before they were quenched, nineteen people had died. One badly burned man staggered to the Tarbell shanty and Mrs.

Tarbell nursed him back to health over the next several weeks.

The demand for Mr. Tarbell's oil tanks grew as oil producers pumped more and more oil from the ground. Three years after settling in the shanty, Mr. Tarbell moved the family to a better house in Rouseville, upon a hillside above the valley of oil derricks and ugliness. Here Ida discovered the shade trees, flowering shrubs, and other greenery that replaced the disorder and danger of the valley below. Also her mother and father helped her develop a taste for literature, music, and the world outside.

Not long afterward oil was discovered near Pithold, ten miles away, and immediately everyone in Rouseville picked up their possessions and rushed to the new location. The Tarbells remained in their new home, but Mr. Tarbell erected a shop in Pithold and continued his business there.

One night he came home, unhitched Flora, his little horse, and fed her. Then he walked slowly into the kitchen, his head bowed sadly. His wife ran to meet him.

"Whatever is wrong?"

"Abraham Lincoln is dead."

The next day Mrs. Tarbell shut up the house and hung black mourning crepe on all the doors. Eight-year-old Ida was mystified. Why this fuss about someone they neither knew nor had ever seen? Certainly it did not concern her. Nevertheless, she never forgot her parents' grief, and many years later she was to find out why they were so upset.

The Tarbell family had grown with the arrival of Sarah and Frankie after Will. Sarah contracted, but managed to fight off, the dreaded scarlet fever. Frankie was less fortunate. Ida stood outside her little brother's room, horrified as she listened to his screaming. She felt so helpless and sorry for him, and then was unable to understand why he had to die.

When Ida was thirteen they moved again, this time to a new house her father had built in Titusville. A hotel there was scheduled to be demolished. Mr. Tarbell had admired its handsome woodwork, long French windows, and lovely wrought iron brackets. He was able to buy the building. He tore it down and used the materials to build a house for his family.

Living in the large town meant Ida no longer attended a small school. Instead she went to the crowded public school and soon became a truant. She felt certain the teacher hardly knew or cared whether or not she was in class. She soon discovered her mistake when her teacher lectured her for truancy. Thereafter she became a model student. In high school Ida made the honor roll each term, feeling she owed this to her parents and teachers.

Ever since she could remember, Ida had collected stones, plants, leaves, insects—anything that caught her attention as she walked outdoors. She saw each of these items only as something to put under a press, into a bottle, or store in a box, certainly not to study. Now as she eagerly read her high school textbooks she became aware of the value of her collections. She decided to become a scientist.

Meanwhile, Mr. Tarbell had realized that wooden oil tanks would soon be obsolete. He had formed a partnership with M.E. Hess as an oil producer. Their little company—and the whole town of Titusville—flourished until around 1872, when the partners were shocked and frightened to learn that a group of companies secretly threatened their business. This combination of companies, known as the South Improvement Company (later Standard Oil Company), represented oil producers like themselves.

The group had persuaded the railroads to haul their oil at much lower rates than other producers had to pay. As if this were not bad enough, the railroads also paid South Improvement a drawback on every barrel of oil shipped by producers like Mr. Tarbell who did not belong to the group. This meant that South Improvement Company could sell its oil for far less than anyone else and eventually would have a monopoly.

When Mr. Tarbell told the family about this unfair and highly dishonest practice, Ida saw clearly that it was wrong. The fact that railroads gave special rates and drawbacks to other industries was commonplace, but that did not make it right. It meant the public paid higher prices, and many small businesses were forced to close. At fifteen Ida realized that people like those controlling South Improvement Company enjoyed special benefits or privileges, and her hatred of privilege was born. However, she was wise enough to know that she could do nothing about it. Instead, she turned her attention to an equally disturbing discovery: that the world was not made in six days, each with twenty-four hours.

She had begun to question some of the teachings of her Methodist church. Books she read in school told that the world was created millions of years ago and that man evolved from lower forms of life. The Bible contradicted this. What was right? Furthermore, she reasoned, if there were this uncertainty about Biblical truth, how could she be sure there was a God?

This doubt and questioning proved a turning point. Hereafter she would seek the truth about any statement or matter that seemed dubious to her. Here was her first challenge: to find out how and when life started. In doing so perhaps she would learn more about God and find Him again.

How to tackle the problem? Would not a microscope provide a solution? Immediately she began to save her allowance. She also begged her parents to let her use the tower room. With windows on three sides, it rose above the house and was reached by steep stairs. Here she placed her desk, her collections, books, and a brand-new microscope. As she peered through the glass she decided she would become a biologist and study plant life, but first she must get a college education so she could become a teacher.

This decision led to another—that she would never marry. Teaching would bring independence and freedom. Marriage would tie her down, prevent her from pursuing her new goal of becoming a biology teacher.

Thus in the fall of 1876, at a time when only a few colleges accepted women students, eighteen-year-old Ida entered Allegheny College, the lone woman in the freshman class of forty-one. Unlike most of her classmates, she started college training with a microscope and a purpose—an earnest search for learning and independence.

Main Street, Titusville, Pennsylvania, in the 1860s

Chapter 3

COLLEGE DAYS

In Meadville, Pennsylvania, at Allegheny College, Ida thought Bentley Hall, with its cupola, was the most beautiful building she had ever seen. There was Culver Hall, a frame building where the men students boarded, and then Ruter Hall, a brick structure that looked more like a factory than a college building.

In Ruter Hall was the library. It was one huge room, its walls lined with books—more books than Ida had ever seen before in her life. During the next four years she would spend many hours there, often perched on top of a ladder, reading a favorite book.

There were few women students. Few colleges admitted women in the 1870s and most people did not approve of women going to college.

One warm day that fall Ida walked across the lawn below Bentley to sit on a bench shaded by a large tree. Suddenly she heard someone shouting at her:

"Come back! Come back quickly!" It was one of the upper-classwomen. "You mustn't go on that side of the walk. Only men go there!"

Ida picked up her books and returned to Bentley, wondering why the college permitted such a stupid rule. Then she decided not to let such childishness bother her. Hadn't she come here for one purpose, to learn all she could about science? Thinking of Professor Jeremiah Tingley, head of the Department of Natural Science, helped her forget the incident. Attending his lectures had become the most exciting experience since she started college.

Best of all she liked to hear Professor Tingley lecture on his faith in nature. He believed in pantheism, which held that God is nature and the whole universe. Ida soon thought of herself as a pantheist and was sure that with the aid of her microscope she would someday discover the true God for herself.

Professor Tingley encouraged his students to read their textbooks and then explore the world. "Go see for yourself," he would say. When he learned of Ida's interest in the microscope, he urged her to use the large binocular instrument the college owned.

"Try everything in the laboratory," he told her. "You may even experiment with the electrical apparatus."

Best of all were the evenings spent in the Tingleys' living room. Here the professor excited a small group of interested students with news of the latest scientific inventions. A few weeks after Ida started college her father took her to the Philadelphia Centennial Exposition, which marked the one-hundredth anniversary of the signing of the Declaration of

Independence. Numerous buildings were filled with exhibits of all kinds showing the progress that had been made in America in science, agriculture, transportation, construction, and many other fields.

When Ida returned, Professor Tingley's first question to her was: "Did you see the telephone?"

Somewhat ashamed, she shook her head. "I never heard of it," she replied.

A few weeks later the professor showed the students a telephone he had just made. "You'll talk to your homes from these rooms one day," he said. Most of the students merely smiled at his words and thought he was a dreamer.

By this time seven female students had their own dormitory, "The Snow Flake," located just behind Culver Hall, the boarding house for male students. Gradually the boys and girls became more friendly, and some of the young men asked the girls to go out with them. Ida found that companionship of boys was fun and soon she was canoeing, hiking, and sleigh riding along the snow-packed roads.

She was not a beautiful girl, but her sparkling eyes, friendly smile, outgoing personality, and willingness to go along with the crowd made her popular. She found the greatest pleasure in having many friends, and did not want just one boy as her special pal.

Members of the various Allegheny fraternities gave their fraternity pins to the girls they especially liked, just as is the custom today. Sometimes it could mean that the couple was engaged to be married. Evidently a number of boys liked Ida, for one morning she entered chapel wearing not one but four different fraternity pins on her coat. The boys who had given them to her were furious and thereafter most fraternity brothers had nothing to do with her.

This bit of thoughtlessness did not dim her popularity, however. During her third year classmates elected her class secretary. She was also an editor of the college newspaper and became an active member of the college literary society.

None of these activities interfered with her studies. Often she rose at four in the morning to study. Her goal was to do her very best at whatever she tackled, to make everything she did as perfect as possible. Many years later when she looked back on her college years, she admitted that she had not gotten as much as she might have from her college studies. She realized it was not the fault of her teachers but that she had not learned how to study.

During the winter of her senior year Ida began to think about what she would do after graduation. If she did not marry, there were only two things a young woman might do. She could become either a missionary or a teacher. Although two ministers pleaded with her to prepare for a life as a missionary somewhere in Africa or Asia, she had no interest in that career. Instead, when she received a letter from the Poland Union Seminary in Poland, Ohio, she eagerly replied, saying she would indeed be interested in the position as "preceptress," or principal teacher. After many letters and an interview, the board of trustees appointed her to the position at an annual salary of $500.

Now she would be on her own. She thought the salary would make it possible to save money so she could continue studying science. Then, perhaps, she would find out how life on earth really began. When she made that discovery, maybe she would find God, too.

That spring Ida and her classmates marched slowly down the aisle toward the stage where the president handed each one a diploma. Ida was one of the more fortunate graduates; she knew what she would be doing once she left Allegheny. The thought of becoming a teacher was exciting and challenging. Someday she might get married, but that was not important at the moment.

Chapter 4

STARTING HER CAREER

Poland was a pleasant town with many comfortable homes and wide lawns. It was surrounded by neat farms with well-kept barns and silos. Aside from a few stores, the town's chief business was the seminary, which served partly as a high school and partly as a college. Such schools soon disappeared and were replaced by four-year colleges.

From the day when she arrived in Poland until two years later when she left the seminary, Ida felt that most of the people were unfriendly to her. What she did not know when she accepted the position was that the woman who had held the job before was well loved by the community. Often people would stop Ida on the street and tell her that Miss Blakesley had taught them and that they felt bad that she would not be there to teach their children. Ida wanted to tell them it was not her fault, but she merely listened and nodded her head.

Even more important, Ida had never been told about the terrible work load she and one assistant would have to undertake. The president, who seemed mostly interested in leading the chapel exercises, refused to teach any classes. He claimed he was much too busy running the school. This left all of the teaching to Ida and the other instructor. Ida began to lose her enthusiasm for the job as she tried to keep up with the teaching schedule. She was expected to teach two classes in each of four languages—Greek, French, German, and Latin—as well as courses in botany, geology, geometry, and trigonometry.

Evenings were spent correcting papers and preparing to teach the next day's classes. Somehow she managed to keep a chapter ahead of her students in all of the language classes, and each night she worked out lectures for the next day in the other subjects.

Had it not been for Clara Walker, or "Dot," as she was called, Ida would never have been able to stay at Poland. During her first week, when she was almost ready to quit, the town banker, Robert Walker, tipped his hat as they met near the school.

"Keep a stiff upper lip!" he said and then walked on. Ida wondered how he knew about her unhappiness.

The following day his daughter, Dot, visited Ida at the seminary and insisted she take time out for a ride in the buggy. Dot knew how hard it must be for a young teacher who had to take the place of the beloved Miss Blakesley.

Clara Walker and Ida became close friends. The good times they shared enabled the new teacher to put up with her heavy work schedule and difficulties in dealing with students.

Ida never forgot the long drives they took into the country-side. In later years she would remember many of those experiences as she wrote about the unfair ways some workers were treated. One night while driving back from Youngs-town, ten miles away, they passed through the furnace dis-trict where iron ore was smelted in the steel-making pro-cess. One of the furnaces had burst, causing molten metal to trap a number of workers. Their charred bodies were being carried across the road just as the two young women approached in their carriage.

Once the two friends went down into a deep coal mine just outside of Poland. The miners lived in little houses nearby and appeared to be very poor. The entrance to the mine shaft was near a farmhouse. When the two women came up from the mine they watched the farmer butcher some of his pigs.

"What are you going to do with all that meat?" Ida asked.

The farmer wiped his hands on his apron and leaned against the smokehouse. "When the mine closes because we can't sell any more coal," he explained, "we've got to help the miners and make certain they have something to eat."

That night as she lay in bed thinking about what she had seen at the farm, Ida realized that she could be much worse off. True, teaching was a disappointment. It was hard work, there was no pleasure in preparing and giving the lessons, and worse yet, her salary was not enough to support her. Without help from her father she would not have been able to finish the second year. Still, she had a job and many college graduates would gladly step into her place.

Not knowing what to do after her two years of teaching, Ida asked her mother if she minded if she came home. "Of course, that is your right," said her mother. Both Ida's parents believed their home should always be open to any relative who had no other place to go.

Ida returned to her beloved tower room and work with her microscope. She began looking through the glass for tiny creatures that she knew were near underground oil fields. Although her research would not help people like her father in the oil business, it was an important part of her searching back into the earth's history that she hoped would someday point the way to discovering God.

Chapter 5

BECOMING A WRITER

One cold Sunday afternoon during the following winter Dr. Theodore L. Flood, a retired Methodist minister, came to call. He was editor of a magazine called *The Chautauquan* that was published in Meadville, where Ida had gone to college.

"Can you help me out?" he asked Ida. "I have a new department for my readers and need someone to work with me for a month or two. It would just be a couple of weeks each month."

"Yes, I'd be glad to," she replied. "What do you want me to do?" The prospect of a little spending money of her own, with plenty of time left over for her microscope, was appealing.

Another reason for her enthusiasm was her familiarity with *The Chautauquan* and the chautauqua movement. Ever since she was a child her family had traveled each summer to the Methodist camp meeting at Fair Point on Lake Chautauqua in New York. The camp was started to give parents a safe place to bring their children for Bible teaching and healthy outdoor recreation. What began as a few cottages and tents soon grew into a large colony of summer cottages, a hotel, theater, and other buildings, some used for classrooms. A high fence surrounded the camp, and all campers and their guests had to have tickets to pass through the gates. No one could enter or leave after ten o'clock at night.

In 1878 Dr. John Vincent, the director of the camp, announced a four-year course of home reading for men and women who had not had a college education. Before that summer was over the Chautauqua Literary and Scientific Circle signed up some eight thousand members, each of whom received one or two carefully chosen books for reading and study every month. Two years later it was decided to publish a monthly magazine, *The Chautauquan*, that would enable the leaders of the circle to keep in touch with the members.

In starting the reading course Dr. Vincent had overlooked an important fact about his members. Most of the men and women who joined the circle did not own dictionaries or reference books. A great many lived on farms and ranches, out in the mountains, and far from libraries. Soon letters were flooding into the office asking questions such as: "How do you pronounce this word?" "Who was this woman?" "Where is that city?" "What is the meaning of this word?"

"Why couldn't *The Chautauquan* take care of these questions?" Dr. Vincent had asked Dr. Flood. "It seems to me that if someone wrote notes about the readings, explaining the meaning of different words, giving pronunciations and other information, our members wouldn't have to write to us. Do you suppose you can find someone to try it out?"

"I'm sure I can," Dr. Flood replied, thinking of Ida Tarbell, and that was why he called on her.

Because the Titusville library was not too well equipped, Ida used Meadville libraries and then decided to stay there while working for Dr. Flood. Soon she was not only annotating *The Chautauquan*'s articles, but learning professional journalism techniques from the printing office foreman, as well as answering Dr. Flood's editorial correspondence. Although this was a big undertaking, she found time to write articles for the magazine, occasionally taking a short trip to obtain information.

One day she read a report about women inventors. It stated that during the forty-five years the United States Patent Office had been open, women had patented only 334 inventions.

"That can't be!" she exclaimed to Dr. Flood. "Think how clever women have had to be in the kitchen and on the farm." Since her teens, Ida had been aware of the women's suffrage movement. She felt strongly about the independence of women, married or single.

She asked if she might take a trip to Washington, D.C. to find out if the information about women's patents were really true.

The following week she walked into the Patent Office. She felt very important but nevertheless frightened by the prospect of having to meet and talk with the director. As soon as she was introduced to him she forgot her fright and explained the purpose of her visit. He showed her the patent files and in a short time she discovered that women had taken out not 334 but over 2,000 patents. She later told about her discovery in an article in the magazine.

Work on *The Chautauquan* stopped near the end of June, since no issues were published in July or August. Instead, Dr. Flood sent his magazine staff, now grown to five women, to Lake Chautauqua. Here they were responsible for publishing an eight-page newspaper, the *Daily Herald*. Ida often wrote several articles for a single issue, one of which always told about what would be happening in camp that day. Interesting speakers and important people came to lecture. Ida met and talked with many of them, and sometimes wrote about her conversations in the newspaper.

Back in Meadville, Ida and the other workers on *The Chautauquan* began to report to their readers about important events happening in the country. In their articles they supported labor's fight for the eight-hour day and higher wages. They discussed the problems of poverty and the growing slum areas in large cities. They argued for better schools and for temperance—a movement that called for the end of selling alcoholic beverages.

As Ida thought and wrote about these and many other subjects, she jotted down ideas in several notebooks. Then drawing on many of these notes, she decided to write a novel about Oil Creek where she had lived as a small child. After struggling with three chapters she gave up, realizing that she was not a novelist.

Next, she began to think about what women had done in government, business, and other fields. Men did not run the world all by themselves, she reasoned. Women, too, had managed to do many important things. Those who excited her most were the brave females who were active in the French Revolution in 1789. She wrote several short articles about them, including one on Madame Roland, who especially interested her. Jeanne Manon Phlipon Roland de la Platière and her husband were leaders of one of the parties (Girondists) active in trying to bring about a change in the French government. They were not successful and as she was led to the guillotine Madame Roland shouted: "O Liberty, what crimes are committed in thy name!" When Ida finished the piece, she felt there were too many important facts that could not be found in any American library. How could she learn more about this woman? The more she thought about her, the more eager she was to learn everything possible.

There was only one way. She must do thorough research, but that could be done only in Paris. How could she, a woman, go and live in a strange country? How could she afford it? She did not want to get a job in France; she wanted to be free to write. Then she had an idea.

She had heard about syndicates, large businesses that bought articles and then sold them for publishing in many newspapers at the same time. That was it! She would become a journalist, write articles about France, and sell them to American syndicates. That would be fun and support her, too.

By now she had tired of working for *The Chautauquan*. Dr. Flood wanted her to direct the publication of his magazine and newspapers. It certainly was a secure job but it offered no chance to travel or do interesting writing. As she thought about her dream of going abroad, she became determined to make it come true.

In her enthusiasm she forgot that she was not a writer and knew nothing about the publishing world. She forgot that she was afraid to meet people. She overlooked the fact that she was now thirty-three, an age that in those days was considered too old to undertake such a venture, especially for a woman. Most important of all, she had not considered her finances realistically; she had barely enough money saved up for such an expensive venture.

She jotted down in her notebook the reasons why she would be successful in doing the kind of journalism on which she had decided. She planned everything before she started to write. She was confident that she could judge what was important about a subject. She felt that she could make her writing fresh and original. Finally, she worked steadily and painstakingly. Surely all these qualities would enable her to become a journalist and sell her articles.

To prepare herself for the trip, Ida realized she must learn to speak French. She had read the language for years but speaking it was another matter. She needed someone to talk with and decided to call on Monsieur Séraphin Claude, an elderly French dyer in Titusville. She told him about her forthcoming trip.

"Would you and your wife be willing to take me as a pupil, say three times a week?" she asked.

The idea delighted the Claudes. During one of the lessons Monsieur Claude told Ida how much he longed to see France again before he died. He insisted that she learn and repeat daily Béranger's poem, "France Adorée," and later when she first saw Paris, she understood why. If only he, too, could visit his beloved homeland!

She traveled to Cincinnati, Pittsburgh, and several other cities to tell newspaper syndicate editors about her plan to live in Paris and write articles about life in France. A half-dozen promised to buy articles at six dollars each.

"How I ever managed to sell them the idea, I can't understand!" she later told her father.

None of her friends agreed with her plan; they thought

she was foolish. Only her mother and father gave her encouragement, although they were fearful that she would not succeed.

"I don't know what you can do, Ida," her father said, "that's for you to decide. If you think you can do it, try it."

Her friends laughed at her, but Josephine Henderson and Mary Henry, who had worked with her on *The Chautauquan*, wanted to go with her. They would help share expenses and, best of all, she would not be alone in a strange land. At the very last moment, just before they climbed the gangplank at New York, Annie Towle, a friend of Mary's, arrived to join them.

The ship's deep whistle sounded four times, the gangplank was raised, and there was no turning back.

Chapter 6

LIFE IN PARIS

Ida knew exactly where she wanted to live in Paris. It would be in the famous Latin Quarter, somewhere near the Musée (Museum) de Cluny. As soon as they arrived Ida took her companions to a cheap hotel. It was agreed they would stay there while they looked for rooms in the Latin Quarter. Every apartment they saw was small, dirty, full of fleas, and run down. Finally, on the third day they rented four garret rooms from a Madame Bonnet. The apartment was clean and contained two tiny bedrooms, a living room, and a kitchen so tiny it held little more than a sink. It was not the glamorous Latin Quarter the four had hoped to find, but they could not afford anything better.

Once they had unpacked their bags, the four friends visited the small shops in the neighborhood. They observed that most of the housewives bought only enough food for one meal at a time. For example: one egg, one roll, and milk for lunch. It was not an easy adjustment for Americans who were used to eating well.

"Why, the very scraps from a meal at home would feed us here," Ida observed one evening as she peered down at her empty plate. In a short time they managed to shop as their neighbors did, a little at a time, and to enjoy it, also. Occasionally they found an attractive but inexpensive restaurant where a good meal cost only a franc, or nineteen cents in their American money.

They were scarcely settled in Madame Bonnet's rooming house when Ida started work. She wrote articles about the everyday life in Paris which so fascinated her. She noticed the cleanliness of the city, what the people ate and drank, how they amused themselves, and many other things. At the end of her first week she mailed two newspaper articles back to the States. She started buying a number of newspapers each day to learn as much as possible about Paris and to furnish ideas and material for her writing. The precious money hidden in her room grew smaller and smaller, a constant reminder that she must keep working and selling to the syndicates.

Each day Ida rose at six and went out to buy breakfast rolls and coffee. Then she usually went to the National Library to do research on Madame Roland and to work on articles. It was quiet there and she could concentrate on her writing. At noon she returned to her apartment for a meager lunch, then spent the afternoon exploring the city, listening to the people, and gathering ideas for her articles. Every so often she mailed what she had written to syndicates, wondering all the time whether she would be able to support herself and stay in France.

Just six weeks after she had carried her luggage off the boat the first check came for a syndicate article. A few days later two more checks arrived. This meant that three of the six newspaper syndicates she had visited had purchased her material. Doubts about her ability to support herself began to disappear.

The best surprise occurred two months later when a letter from Edward Burlingame, editor of *Scribner's Magazine*, brought the almost unbelievable news that he was buying her story, "France Adorée," for one hundred dollars! This story was based on her experience with Monsieur Claude who longed so to see his homeland again.

She could hardly wait to tell the news to the others. Mary was so excited that she suggested they immediately move to a better rooming house. Nothing would have pleased Ida more, but she refused to consider the suggestion. It was not likely she would sell another story for many months, if ever. The one hundred dollars would have to last a long time.

Ida's joy at this sale was quickly shattered. A letter from Titusville made her feel guilty for being so happy and away from home where she was needed. Her sister was in the hospital, her mother was exhausted from worry, and her father's oil business was failing. In spite of all this trouble there was not the slightest hint that Ida should come home. Her family was very supportive of her venture. Nevertheless, Ida imagined herself a deserter but knew she must stay in Paris. Yes, she reasoned, all would be well if she worked hard, made a lot of money, and sent her family large checks from time to time.

Anxious to broaden their contacts with the Parisians, the four women became active at the McCall Mission, run by Americans. It fed, clothed, and cared for the poor, and its leaders also conducted religious services. Soon the women met a group of young American students from Johns Hopkins University in Baltimore, Maryland. As Ida and her friends spent more and more evenings and weekends with these students, they gradually withdrew from their work at the McCall Mission. These new friends were full of gaiety that helped Ida overcome her shyness. Soon she was able to enter into the fun, and even participate in a practical joke now and then.

Once winter had spread over Europe, living in a garret room lost its romance. Ida burned only as much coal in her grate as she felt she could afford. She bought thick-soled shoes to keep her feet warm and dry, and slipped into her sealskin coat when she went to bed. One cold after another made it difficult to keep up her heavy schedule. After she had suffered a stomachache for some time, she gave up milk because she thought it unsafe and drank only coffee instead.

The spring of 1892 brought great change. The weather grew warm and in May when Paris looked its best, her "France Adorée" was published. Many of the Americans who lived nearby saw the story in *Scribner's Magazine* and came to visit her. They became interested in her plans for a biography of Madame Roland and begged Ida to give lectures about the famous woman. Far from pleasing her, however, this added chore of having to prepare speeches, as well as write articles for five to ten dollars apiece (if the editors bought them), depressed her. She wondered whether the hard work and poverty were worth it. Had she been wise to venture out on her own? Could she really succeed in supporting herself? The most important question that troubled her was: How could she become a scholar, study, and spend more time on the French Revolution?

Her gloom and fears disappeared unexpectedly when Mr. Burlingame made an unexpected visit while staying in Paris. After they had talked for a few minutes, Ida could feel her stomach tighten as she leaned forward, swallowed hard, and asked:

"Mr. Burlingame, would Scribner's be interested in publishing a book about Madame Roland—that is, if it turned out to be a good piece of work?"

"I really don't know," he replied. "The suggestion would have to be considered in New York." It was enough of a promise to settle the question that had been troubling her. With the possibility of her book being published, she could continue her writing for the syndicates and also work on her Roland biography.

Another reason for her decision was that the important and popular McClure Syndicate of New York City had purchased the very first article she had submitted. The editor liked it so much he asked for more. By the time Mr. Burlingame came to see her, Ida was selling steadily to this syndicate and had just received a suggestion that she write a series of sketches about French women writers.

The first Sunday of June, 1892, was a day Ida never forgot. Just after she finished her rolls and coffee she felt as though a black cloud had passed before her eyes. Suddenly she knew that a terrible disaster was taking place somewhere. The feeling was so real and upsetting that she could not work, so she walked about the city all day. Late in the afternoon, as she returned home, she stopped to buy a newspaper.

As she stared at the front-page article she saw the reason for her fright. According to the story, Titusville and nearby Oil City had been destroyed by fire and a flood. Only the railroad station and a foundry were left standing. One hundred fifty people had drowned or died in fires.

"That explains my black day," Ida told a friend who had come along and was peering over her shoulder. "My family is dead, our home is gone." She knew it was useless to send a cable. The newspaper told of telegraph wires in the area being knocked down.

That night she hardly slept. The next morning as she was

getting dressed, Madame Bonnet ran up the stairs waving an envelope.

"A cablegram for mademoiselle," she called. Trembling with fear, Ida leaned against the wall as she tore it open. It was from her brother and contained but one word: "Safe."

When a letter from home finally came, she was relieved to learn that her family was safe and their home still standing.

Not long after this experience her roommates returned to the States. At first Ida missed them, but now she was free of all distractions, interruptions, and constant talking. She could be alone in her room and come or go as she pleased.

Madame Bonnet had bought a new house and Ida rented the smallest room. It was a great improvement over the garret. She had lace curtains at the windows, a large velvet chair, a huge desk, and a small closet. The balcony served as a cooler for food during the winter.

Before she had much time to enjoy her new freedom, there was an exciting visit from a man who ran up the four flights of stairs, watch in hand, to breathlessly knock on her door. The arrival of Samuel S. McClure, founder of the McClure Syndicate, was an event that would completely change Ida Tarbell's life and career.

Chapter 7

FAREWELL TO FRANCE

Samuel S. McClure started the McClure Syndicate with his wife, Hattie, as his assistant. Once the business began to grow, Hattie stayed home to raise their family while McClure contacted authors and arranged to buy stories and articles. His goal was to find the very best writers. When his college friend John Phillips came seeking a job, McClure hired him to run the office. This freed McClure to travel, visit authors, and read a half-dozen newspapers plus innumerable articles each day, as well as several books each week.

One day as McClure was standing by John Phillips's desk, he glanced down at an article entitled "The Paving of Paris by Monsieur Alphand." It was a story, submitted by Ida, about Jean Alphand and his services to Paris. McClure was fascinated and read the whole article as he stood there.

He turned to Phillips. "Who is this Ida Tarbell?"

"I have no idea," Phillips replied, and added that he thought she might be a schoolteacher, judging by her handwriting.

"She can write," McClure said and then told Phillips he wanted her to do some writing for the magazine he was planning to start soon.

A few months later McClure arrived in Paris and hurried to the Latin Quarter.

"I've just ten minutes," he told Ida when she opened the door to her apartment. "Must leave for Switzerland tonight."

Ida invited him in and soon McClure was telling her the story of his life, how he met and married Hattie, started the syndicate, and hired John Phillips. Many years later, Ida wrote in her autobiobraphy: "John, always John this, John that, and last a magazine to be—soon. And here I was to come in."

As McClure talked with her, Ida noticed that he was a slender man with a shock of sandy hair and sparkling blue eyes. He seemed charged with electricity—always enthusiastic, tireless, and ever on the go. She liked him from the first time they met.

Then McClure sought her opinion about an article he was planning to publish. He wanted to test her skills as an editor. He liked what she said and asked her to return immediately to the United States to help him start the magazine.

Return to America now! Ida stiffened. She was in the midst of her Roland book. She couldn't give that up.

"Think about it," McClure said when he realized that she would not leave Paris immediately. He explained that he would be needing articles for his new publication. "I particularly want you to write about great English and French scientists," he told her. "Perhaps the first should be Louis

Pasteur, who lives here in Paris. After Pasteur there'll be others."

Although he did not mention it to Ida at the time, there is no doubt that while in Paris McClure sensed the excitement over the renewed interest in Napoleon Bonaparte. A hundred years before, following the revolution in which Madame Roland died, Napoleon had started his rise to power. At one point he became master of all Europe except the British Isles. Ida was also aware of how proud the French were of "the Little Corporal," as he was often called because of his small stature.

Suddenly McClure looked at his watch and jumped up. Instead of ten minutes, they had talked for three hours.

"I must go! Can you lend me forty dollars? It's too late to get to a bank and I must catch that train for Geneva."

Fortunately Ida had exactly forty dollars saved up for a vacation she had planned. It was in her desk and she gave it to him, positive she would never see it again.

"How queer that you should have that much money in the house," McClure said as he took the bills.

"Isn't it?" Ida agreed. "It never happened before."

He thanked her, rushed down the stairs, and out of the building.

Once he had left, Ida regretted her foolishness in giving him the money. Now she would have to forget the vacation. "Serves me right," she thought.

But she was wrong. That night before the train left, McClure wired his brother in their London office to send forty dollars to Ida. A check came shortly thereafter.

As soon as she returned from her vacation, Ida visited Louis Pasteur at the institute he had founded four years earlier. Pasteur had trained to be a chemist and became interested in studying bacteria—tiny microscopic organisms that can be beneficial or harmful. He found that they were responsible for fermenting wine and beer. After much experimenting he developed a heating process to preserve wine, beer, and also milk. Bringing the liquid to 140 or 155 degrees Fahrenheit kills the bacteria and prevents fermentation. This process is known as pasteurization; today most milk is pasteurized.

Ida met Madame Pasteur and her husband in their apartment at one end of the institute. The large rooms had thick curtains, soft dark rugs, and heavy furniture according to the style of the time.

Louis Pasteur's bright eyes sparkled as he received the American writer. Pasteur wanted to know why Ida had come to see him. She explained that Samuel McClure had asked for an article about and pictures of the Pasteurs. There was to be a series of portraits of the scientist from the time he was born until the present.

The Pasteurs were delighted at the request. Madame Pasteur brought out some old photograph albums from which they selected a number of pictures. When the article appeared the following year, Ida took a copy of the magazine to the couple. "He was as pleased as a boy with the pictures," she wrote later.

In addition to Louis Pasteur, Ida interviewed other scientists and several women writers. By this time she had become well known for her writing and had many friends among important families. Her real interest, though, was her biography of Madame Roland. She spent as much time as she could on the project, hoping to finish it before Mr. McClure might start publishing his magazine and beg her to come back to the United States.

In doing her Roland research Ida discovered that her daily walk to the National Library was similar to the route Madame Roland took almost a hundred years before. Ida passed the house where the famous woman was born, the church where she had received her first communion, and the prison where she spent her last days.

"What luck, what luck," Ida would say to herself, "that I should be taking the very walk she took." Nothing had changed over the years and it was easy for Ida to imagine Madame Roland hurrying ahead of her along these same narrow streets.

One day she had an unexpected bit of good fortune. Ida was introduced to Madame Roland's great-granddaughter, Madame Marillier. She and her friends made it possible for

Ida to be the first person to study a large collection of Roland manuscripts in the National Library. This gave her much valuable information. Just as important was Madame Marillier's invitation to spend two weeks with her at Le Clos, the country estate that had been in the Roland family for over two hundred years.

After a long train trip and an hour's ride bumping up and down hills and across fields in a horse cart, they reached the white chateau. It had red tiled roofs, corner towers, a courtyard on one side, and a large garden on the other. From the garden Ida could see a series of hills and valleys that stretched all the way to the lofty Swiss Alps.

The chateau was much the same as when Madame Roland spent four years there with her husband. Most of the rooms were filled with old and valuable books. Ida and Madame Marillier looked through them, hoping to find comments Madame Roland might have written here and there. They also searched desks and bureaus, finding many notes and interesting articles, which later proved of great value for the book.

Ida was permitted to sleep in Madame Roland's bed as well as to handle her jewels and clothing. As she studied the woman's private papers, Ida's admiration began to fade. She learned, among other disturbing facts, that before the Revolution Madame Roland had tried to persuade the king to give her a title. Apparently she was little better than a "glory seeker." It was most disappointing, but Ida decided that she must tell the truth and show the woman exactly as she was. In doing this she did not follow the custom of the time that biographers only praise the people about whom they wrote.

Once Ida had returned to Paris that summer of 1893, she felt that she had finished her research and was ready to start writing. First she had to figure some way to obtain money for food and rent. The money McClure owed her for articles had not come. Just as he had started his new *McClure's Magazine,* the stock market crashed and depression gripped the United States. Some eight thousand businesses and banks closed. Thousands lost their jobs, and armies of the unemployed marched on Washington. McClure simply did not have any money to send to Ida or his other writers.

She was too proud to ask Madame Marillier for a loan. Nor would she admit to her American friends that she needed money. Her solution was to pawn her good sealskin coat. The following month her family sent twenty-five dollars and later she began to receive checks again. It would be possible to stay on in Paris until the spring of 1894.

McClure sent her to Glasgow to interview a Scottish clergyman. During his next trip to France, McClure visited her again. He praised her work and promised to pay what he owed. Then he told her that if she joined his staff in October of the following year, he would send money for her trip back to America and pay her a salary of forty dollars a week.

Her plan now was to return to Titusville, spend several months with her family, and finish the Roland book before October. Then she would try to convince Mr. Burlingame that Scribner's should publish it. She would start working for *McClure's* and make arrangements to write a number of articles about the French for the magazine. Having done that, she would return to Paris and her favorite place, the Latin Quarter. She would take an apartment where she could look out over the rooftops of Paris. There she would spend her time writing for *McClure's* and *Scribner's*, as well as studying the nature of revolutions and trying to learn what women really had contributed to the world.

Certain that she would carry out this plan, she packed her bags and arranged for her return to America. As the steamship pulled away from the dock, she silently said not "goodbye" to the receding French coast, but "au revoir" ("till I see you again").

A woodcut of Ida Tarbell

Chapter 8

IDA TARBELL BECOMES FAMOUS

It was a hot August day in Titusville when Mrs. Tarbell called up to the tower room where Ida was working.

"Mail, Ida. A letter for you. Postmark's New York."

Ida ran downstairs and tore open the envelope; it was from Sam McClure. Short and to the point, it said that he wanted her to come to work as quickly as possible. There was an emergency.

"I'll have to leave as soon as I can get my things together," Ida told her mother. "Must be something important if Mr. McClure needs me there so soon."

She took the train to New York and met McClure at his office. He told her a subscriber to *McClure's* had suggested that the magazine run pictures of Napoleon.

McClure immediately had contacted Gardiner Hubbard, a retired lawyer living in Washington, who had collected valuable portraits of Napoleon. Mr. Hubbard agreed to let McClure use them provided he approved of the articles to accompany them.

"I asked Robert Sharard, one of our English writers, to do articles to go with the engravings we plan to use," he told Ida. "But Sharard's pieces were too hard on Napoleon. Hubbard didn't like them and wouldn't let me use his pictures. So this is where you come in." He paused to wipe his perspiring face, then continued.

"I want you to do a series of articles on Napoleon. Later we'll publish them as a book. When I tell you we've already announced they'll start appearing in our November issue, you'll understand why this is so urgent." He leaned forward. "Tell me, will you do it?"

"Yes, indeed," she answered. "I'll write it but I'll have to go right back to Paris. Where else could I get enough material?"

"We'll see," McClure said, "but you must go to Washington, see the engravings, and talk with Mr. Hubbard before you do anything else. Then we'll discuss Paris and the writing."

McClure introduced Ida to John Phillips, who impressed her as being a very serious man. His spectacles, dark moustache, and pinched mouth made him appear almost unfriendly at first, but Ida soon found that this was not so.

A few days later Ida stood at the front door of the Hubbards' summer home, Twin Oaks, named for two huge trees that grew in front of the magnificent house. It was the largest country estate in the Washington area. Ida soon discovered it to be the most beautiful home she had ever entered. She was not used to such large, tastefully furnished rooms, or servants, including maids, butlers, and gardeners.

Mrs. Hubbard, a gracious woman, greeted Ida and introduced her husband, an elderly but energetic man. He told

Ida they wanted her to stay at Twin Oaks while she worked so that he could keep track of her progress on the book.

Ida immediately began a search to see what material might be available in Washington. She quickly found there was enough in the State Department and the Library of Congress. It was not necessary to go to Paris, so she started work at a desk in a corner of the Library of Congress. Often she continued her writing at night back in her room at Twin Oaks.

From time to time McClure came down unexpectedly from New York for a meeting at the Hubbards' home. He would burst into the formal living room and run about spreading out proofs of pictures on the valuable carpets and furniture. Such behavior so horrified Ida that the first time she apologized for what McClure had done to the room.

Mrs. Hubbard did not mind, though. She laughed and said, "That eagerness of his is beautiful. I am accustomed to geniuses."

Within six weeks the first of the series of Napoleon articles was ready. As soon as Mr. Hubbard approved it, McClure rushed the manuscript back to the New York printing plant while Ida started on the next installment. Later she referred to her work as "biography on the gallop."

This "living sketch" of a great man, as McClure referred to it, was an immediate success. *McClure's* circulation shot from 24,500 to over 65,000 after the first part appeared. By the time the series was completed, there were more than 100,000 readers! While Ida's biography of Napoleon was appearing, McClure was also running short stories and articles by some of America's best-known writers, which also helped build the readership. Nevertheless, Ida Tarbell was the chief attraction.

Newspapers all over the country praised Ida. The *New York Press* called her series "the best short life of Napoleon we have ever seen." Even authorities on Napoleon's life had nothing but good to say about what she had written. The older expensive magazines of quality, such as the *Atlantic, Century, Harper's,* and *Scribner's,* had reason to worry. *McClure's,* which sold for only ten cents, was publishing outstanding articles, too. Ida Tarbell's name was becoming magic!

The editor at Scribner's book publishers had laid Ida's manuscript on Madame Roland on the bottom shelf of his bookcase. He had been certain that no one would buy a book written by an unknown author about an equally unknown foreigner who had died a hundred years before. But now, as he saw that Ida Tarbell was becoming one of the best-known writers in the country, he decided to publish her Roland book.

Now that she had become famous, Ida felt it time to stop and think about her future. Instead of wanting to be free, as she had when she first went to France, she realized that there was great satisfaction and safety in receiving that weekly forty-dollar paycheck. McClure promised to raise her salary and she was sure he would keep his word. Right now it would be more sensible to stay in Washington and New York than return to Europe. Thanks to her work on Napoleon, she had met most of the important literary figures in Washington and was a frequent visitor in many of their homes.

Best of all, she had to admit to herself, she enjoyed the excitement of being part of the *McClure's* staff. The men had taken her, a mere woman, in as one of them. She found them to be good friends and comrades. How fortunate to be in her position! She could not find three more different or fascinating people than Samuel McClure, John Phillips, and August F. Jaccaci, the magazine's art director.

McClure, whom she had known since that afternoon in her Latin Quarter apartment, was always on the go. He was forever thinking ahead to what would interest and excite his readers. Ever ready to try new ideas, he was constantly searching for something new. He called it "creative editing," not done sitting at a desk, but by following scents and hunting, like a dog.

John S. Phillips, McClure's old college friend, was quite the opposite. All day and sometimes into the evening he sat before his old-fashioned rolltop desk. He acted as editor, handled subscriptions, reviewed and signed advertising contracts, watched over the money and accounting, and kept informed about every part of the business. Late in the 1890s he convinced McClure they should have their own printing plant with the latest equipment. McClure left all the details of running the business to Phillips.

Ida had first met August F. Jaccaci, an artist and the art director, while she was living in Paris. He had taken her to dinner to talk about possible articles for the new magazine. Later he sent a cablegram from London telling her to meet him at 5:30 the next morning in the railroad station. He wanted to show her the first issue of *McClure's*. She walked across Paris to meet him and share coffee at a sidewalk café. He could be a charming and lovable man but at times would fly into frightful rages. These fits of anger would come and go, Ida said, "like terrible summer thundershowers."

It was fun and exciting to work with these men. It would be stupid not to stay on and the more she thought about it, she realized how lucky she was to have this opportunity.

Best of all she liked the fact that these men were so soft-hearted. McClure would help anyone who came to him with a hard luck story, and he was forever giving people jobs. Phillips was no different. He was always helping people in trouble. No matter how busy McClure and Phillips might be, they could find time to help someone who needed assistance.

Although the men were kind and generous to others, they

could bicker, be sharp and disagreeable with each other. McClure was a doer who made quick decisions and would try anything new no matter how impractical it might be. Phillips, on the other hand, was a good businessman, never hasty in making a decision, and always careful. The two men often disagreed and Phillips did his best to keep McClure from making bad mistakes and spending too much money.

Phillips may have thought that 100,000 subscribers were more than ample, but McClure looked upon this growth as only the beginning. It was *not* enough, he told the staff. What he wanted now was another series of articles like those on Napoleon to bring in even more readers. He needed another "howler" to do this and he was determined to have his way.

Suddenly he had an idea and sent for Ida Tarbell.

The Bonta House (left) was a hotel that had been
built at an original cost of $80,000. Ida's father had
admired its handsome woodwork, long French
windows, and lovely wrought iron brackets. So he
bought the building for $600, tore it down, and used
the material to build the family's new house (right) in
Titusville.

A street in Paris in the 1860s

Left: Samuel McClure, founder of the McClure Syndicate

Below: Some of the magazines published monthly in New York City at the end of the nineteenth century. *McClure's Magazine* is in the last row.

Ida, her mother, and her sister Sarah seated on the steps of the family home

During World War I, Ida worked on the Women's
Committee of the Council of National Defense.

Ida had lengthy, and sometimes heated, interviews
with Henry Rogers (above) at the Standard Oil
Building at 26 Broadway in New York City (right)
when she was researching her exposé of the
Standard Oil Company.

Chapter 9

HER FIRST LINCOLN BIOGRAPHY

"You wanted to talk with me, Mr. McClure?" Ida asked as she entered his office. It was February, 1895 and she was working on the final Napoleon article.

"Yes, yes," he replied impatiently. "Come in and sit down. I want to talk with you about Abraham Lincoln. He's been dead almost thirty years, you know." Ida nodded and wondered what he would say next.

"I have no doubt," he continued, "that the most important influence in American life since the Civil War has been the life and character of Abraham Lincoln."

He told Ida that he had examined the back files of several magazines and was surprised to find that some of them had never run a single article on the president. "People never have enough about Lincoln," he declared, "and that's what I have in mind for you to do."

McClure was positive that there was a great amount of unpublished material relating to Lincoln. Many of the stories told about him had never been written down. Hundreds of men and women who had known him and worked with him were still alive. These included members of his cabinet, congressmen, editors of great newspapers, lawyers who had worked with him, and countless individuals who were children when Lincoln lived in Illinois and ran for office.

"But several histories have already been published," Ida protested. "What about the ten-volume *Abraham Lincoln: A History*? Wasn't that work written by his secretaries, John Hay and John Nicolay?"

"Of course, of course, and there's the book his law partner, William Herndon, published, plus a lot more, too. All the more reason to do something different—better! I want you to find out what people remember about Lincoln and put it together in several articles. How about it, now? Out with you—look, see, report!"

As McClure was talking, Ida became increasingly upset. "If you once get into American history," she thought, "you know well enough that will finish France." She realized it also would end her search to solve the woman question and discover the nature of revolutions, just as the trip to France had ended work with the microscope and her search for God. Was she going to spend her whole life running from this to that, never settling down to one job? Probably, but when McClure mentioned that he would increase her yearly salary from $2,000 to $5,000, that decided it. She felt it her duty to earn that larger salary and help her family.

"All right, I'll do it," she said, "but I still have Napoleon to finish."

"You're ahead of schedule," McClure reminded her. "You

can get started on Lincoln. We don't want to waste any time."

Her first step was to visit John Nicolay. She asked if there was anything he could give her for a beginning, any stories, letters, or speeches that he and Hay had not used in their book. Mr. Nicolay told her there was nothing at all of any importance to be had. He and Hay had gathered everything together. Then he urged her not to go forward with such a difficult task. "Furthermore," he said, "if you write a popular life on Lincoln, it would decrease the value of our history."

Ida disagreed and said that anything she might do would make more people interested in the subject and there would be more buyers for his book.

Nicolay was not impressed. After all, he told her, there was nothing more to be said or written about Lincoln. Furthermore she would be interfering with his property, stealing his rights. She should not write another book.

Instead of discouraging Ida, Nicolay made her even more determined to undertake the job. He had no right to stop others from writing about Lincoln. She would research her book differently and show Nicolay what she could do!

She decided to start her journey in Knob Creek, Kentucky, near Lincoln's childhood home, and travel wherever he had gone during his lifetime. She would see for herself the places where he had lived, talk with the people who knew him. As she traveled she would search through country histories, newspapers, and courthouses. She would pick up pictures where she could, and, if she were lucky, might discover letters or stories that were not already in Nicolay's books.

McClure saw her off on the start of her first trip to Kentucky. It was a cold day and he was concerned.

"Have you warm bed socks?" he wanted to know. "We'll send you some if not. It will be awful in those Kentucky hotels." She soon found that he was right, but she kept moving from one place to another in spite of cold dingy hotels and trains.

What surprised Ida was that most men and women hardly remembered Lincoln. A few said they knew he was a special person. Many still could not understand how someone who was a friend or neighbor could have become president of the United States. As she hurried about the countryside asking questions, people looked upon her as a curiosity. A woman did not travel alone in those days; certainly she did not seek information about a president who had died some thirty years before.

Ida returned to New York with little to show for her efforts. True, she had found a newspaper article here and there, an odd picture, a letter or two, and had written down a few stories that people had told her. Still, there was nothing unusual or noteworthy. She met with McClure and Phillips and soon they agreed that it was not possible to do the articles based on what people remembered about the president. Instead, Ida should include the small items she had gathered in a brand new life of Lincoln, using information already published.

Mrs. Emily Lyons, whom Ida had met in Washington, learned about the Lincoln book. Mrs. Lyons lived in Chicago and insisted Ida come to her home there.

"I'll see that you meet Robert Lincoln, and I'll see that he gives you something," she promised.

When Ida arrived at Mrs. Lyons's home, she was introduced to Lincoln's son, Robert. Then Mrs. Lyons served tea and as she filled the cups she turned to Mr. Lincoln.

"Now, Robert, I want you to give her something worthwhile."

Ida was so overwhelmed to be drinking tea with Abraham Lincoln's son that she hardly heard him reply, "Of course, if you say so, Emily." Then he told Ida that he had nothing that would really help her because everything he had ever seen had either been taken away or already used by other writers. However, there was one item she could have. He thought it was the first picture ever taken of his father. It had never been published and he would be glad to let her have it.

This find proved one of the most important during the four years Ida spent writing the book. The picture revealed not the rude, shabby, ungainly man who often is shown in history books. Instead, it was the photo of a handsome young man with the familiar Lincoln face but without its sadness. This Lincoln had a dreamy look.

Although this was all Robert Lincoln gave Ida, nothing could have done more for the success of the undertaking. In November, 1895, ten months after she started work on the book, the first part appeared in *McClure's* with the picture of young Lincoln on the cover. More than 175,000 subscribers awaited the start of the biography; the next month some 250,000 people were subscribing to the magazine so they would not miss a single issue!

Every day mailmen lugged huge bags of letters to the office. People from all parts of the country offered information, asked questions, invited Ida to come visit them, or wrote to tell how much they had loved Lincoln.

Ida continued her search for information, traveling, researching, visiting, calling on people, and writing; she was constantly on the go. As soon as she finished a chapter, McClure read it three times. If the third reading did not interest him, Ida had to rewrite it. He wanted everything in his magazine to be lively and at the same time present the better side of life.

The series stretched to twenty articles over four years and later appeared as a two-volume book. Ida did meticulous research and checked and double-checked facts.

She was considered an authority of the life of Abraham Lincoln. In 1924 her book *In the Footsteps of the Lincolns*, which traced the history of the Lincoln family, was published.

While she was writing the Lincoln biography McClure asked Ida to help Charles Dana. The famous editor of the *New York Sun* needed someone to write a book about the Civil War for him. Dana had been in the War Department and although he was an excellent editor, he was not a writer. He promised to give his whole war story to *McClure's* if Ida would review the documents, talk with him, and do the writing. Although she disliked Dana, she agreed to do it. The book carried Dana's name as author and was highly praised, but Ida received no credit for what she had done.

All this work, travel, meetings, and endless correspondence finally wore down the active woman. During the summer of 1896 she was so exhausted that she entered the Clifton Springs Sanitarium near Rochester, New York. It was the only way she could get a complete rest. For the next thirty years she returned there annually to get away from the world.

When she came back to New York she resumed her busy schedule, traveling between New York and Washington, west to Illinois to look for Lincoln documents, and east again to Washington. Occasionally McClure would send for her, saying he must see her immediately. She would drop everything, take the first train to New York, and often find that he had just left town. It was an exhausting life, but she loved it.

By the turn of the century—1900—McClure was making it possible for rich and poor alike to read good literature. He did this by charging only ten cents for the magazine and publishing articles and stories written by many of America's foremost writers. Three of them were Lincoln Steffens, William Allen White, and Ray Stannard Baker, all former newspaper reporters. They would soon become especially important to *McClure's*. Together with Ida Tarbell, they would bring to the magazine a new kind of reporting.

This change occurred one day after McClure told his staff that something was missing from the magazine. Like a citizen, it too must take an active part in the world. It could not vote or hold office, but it could inform Americans about both the good and the bad in their country. *McClure's* would become a more useful publication if it brought important information to its readers. Hereafter this was what he expected.

About this same time Ida was spending more time in Washington. She wanted to learn all she could about the city and the government. She noticed that most of the men and women in federal service were devoted to their work. They were serving their fellow Americans.

Weren't many of America's problems here too? she asked herself. Dishonest businessmen were cheating their customers. Some corporations were charging the public higher prices than necessary. Other companies were selling meat, milk, and various foods that were prepared in filthy factories and were dangerous to the public health. Corrupt politicians were cheating the public and rewarding their friends. Even though she was not working for the government, Ida became convinced that she should do something to help end these wrongs.

As she thought about this she had no idea that her next assignment at *McClure's* would give her an opportunity to serve others, and in so doing become even more famous. Once again she would be running from this to that, but this time it would be for the benefit of everyone, not just herself.

A photograph of Ida Tarbell taken in about 1902.

Chapter 10

STANDARD OIL COMPANY

The *McClure's* staff discussed the trusts that were forcing small businesses to close. Ida suggested they do a series of articles on the sugar trust that had forced the price of sugar sky-high. McClure said that was not important enough. Then they talked about the beef trust that had gobbled up all the meat packers in the Middle West. But when Philip Armour, leader of the trust, died shortly thereafter, they dropped that idea. Ray Stannard Baker then proposed he look into the powerful United States Steel Corporation, which acted like a trust. In November, 1901 his article "What the U.S. Steel Corp. Really Is" appeared. Baker showed how J. Pierpont Morgan, the powerful Wall Street banker, controlled the steel company and how it operated according to its own rules and regulations, paying no attention to the laws of the land.

This was the start of what McClure wanted, but in the meantime he had gone to Europe for his health. Phillips was seeking something even more important. One morning Ida told him about her father's oil tank business, how he had become a small oil producer, and then was put out of business by Rockefeller's South Improvement Company (now

Standard Oil Company). As she explained how the trust worked, she became excited over the idea of writing a history of the Rockefeller company herself. She knew that she could do it but thought that no one would want to read it.

Phillips urged her to prepare an outline of her history and then take it to McClure. Such an important series of articles would require his approval. She made her outline and went directly to Lausanne, Switzerland, where McClure and his wife, Hattie, were taking a rest cure. There Ida found that McClure did not want to look at her outline.

"Let's have some fun first." McClure had become bored with the rest cure. "We'll all go to Greece for the winter." Instead of traveling directly there he led them to Lake Lucerne, Milan, and Venice. Then he decided that Hattie needed another cure before they went to Greece, so they stopped at the Italian spa of Salsomaggiore. There, as they took mud and steam baths, he studied the outline and discussed the project with Ida.

"It will be easy to get the necessary documents and study them," Ida assured McClure. "There have been many governmental investigations and reports."

"You go back to New York and see what you can make of the outline," McClure finally told her. Shortly thereafter Ida was at her desk laying out her plans.

Everyone who learned of her ideas tried to dissuade her. Standard Oil had made people afraid of its power.

"Don't do it, Ida. They will ruin the magazine," her father told her.

Others warned that if she went ahead the company would surely "get" her in one way or another. None of this scare talk frightened Ida or Phillips. She was going to do honest research to find out how a trust started and worked. She was not accusing Rockefeller of doing anything illegal. She was merely searching for facts. Actually she suspected that Rockefeller might not have done anything illegal.

Once Ida started traveling in search of books, documents, letters, and governmental reports, she discovered that many had disappeared. It looked as though some had been destroyed or bought up by agents of Standard Oil. Even unprinted court records had been stolen from the files and could not be found. The more she searched the more suspicious the trust appeared.

Since Cleveland had been the home of Standard Oil for so many years, Ida decided to hire someone there to help her research local libraries, court records, and government files. She found a young associate editor of *The Chautauquan*, John M. Siddall, who wanted nothing more than to help her. He proved so useful and bright that McClure told Ida he wanted "Sid" in the magazine office as soon as she could let him go.

Ida and Sid worked for about a year before McClure announced that a series of articles on the oil trust would begin appearing soon in *McClure's*. Then there was another of those unexpected surprises that Ida had frequently experienced.

This time the surprise was that Samuel Clemens, the author famous as Mark Twain, would enable Ida to meet with a top officer of Standard Oil. Clemens's good friend Henry Rogers, a Standard Oil official, had heard about Ida's forthcoming history and had asked Clemens to find out about it.

"Why not let Ida tell him herself?" McClure asked, and she agreed.

Early in January, 1902, Ida went to Henry Rogers's home in midtown Manhattan. Her knees were trembling slightly as she rang the bell. She had never before met such an important businessman. What would he say? Would he threaten her?

A maid led her into the attractive library and then Mr. Rogers stepped in. He was quite tall, handsome, and well dressed. A drooping white moustache hid his mouth. He was cordial to Ida and she realized that he wanted her to feel at ease. He asked where she had first become interested in the oil business.

"On the flats and hills of Rouseville," she replied.

"Of course! Of course! I remember your father's tank shop." Then the two of them started chatting about those early days when they both lived on Oil Creek. Rogers had married and bought a home there when he had gone into the oil business. At first he had fought Mr. Rockefeller's South Improvement Company, then joined it, and later rose to an important position in Standard Oil.

Next he wanted to know why Ida had not come to Standard Oil when she started her history. She laughed and replied that she knew it would be useless, no one would tell her anything.

"We've changed our policy," Rogers assured her. "We are giving out information." He told her about the company, how it had started, and all the great things it had done. As they talked Ida relaxed and enjoyed their discussion.

They agreed that Ida would come to his office in the Standard Oil building downtown at 26 Broadway whenever she had something to ask him. He would give her everything she needed to broaden her understanding. However, she told him, she would still feel free to use her own judgment in what she wrote. He nodded in agreement.

During the next two years Ida made frequent visits to the downtown building. Her visits were kept a secret. She would be led in by a route that made certain no one saw her entering Rogers's office, and when she left she was guided to the elevators by another way. One mystery she never solved concerned the man who always was sitting across the courtyard staring at her whenever she was with Rogers. The only other person whom she met was Miss Harrison, Rogers's secretary, who appeared only if Rogers needed a document from the files.

All of their talks were easy and natural. Occasionally they argued and one of them would be angry for a moment. Then the subject would be changed. Once Ida exploded and told Rogers that the man about whom they were talking was a liar, and she added, "you know it."

Mr. Rogers looked out the window, pretending to be observing the weather. "I think it is going to rain" was his only comment.

He was able to show her documents and also was able to let her talk to many of the people whom she wished to see. One of them was Henry Flagler, one of the organizers of the South Improvement Company. A close friend and associate of Rockefeller, he became very wealthy and owned the Florida East Coast Railway, steamship lines, and luxurious hotels in Florida. Ida was especially anxious to learn whether it was Flagler who first suggested forcing all the other oil companies out of business. Instead of answering her question, he told her the story of his life. She tried once again, but he avoided answering and she realized that it was hopeless.

One day Ida showed Rogers the record of a court hearing at which he had not told the truth. When she asked him to explain why he lied in court, he shrugged and said that she had no business asking about his private affairs. When she asked him what right his company had to take rebates from the railroads on shipments of other companies' oil, he smiled and explained that if Standard Oil had not taken the rebates, someone else would have.

She tried to find out why, instead of acting dishonestly, they did not insist on everyone being honest with each other. His answer was simply that there is always someone in business who is dishonest and one of the other smaller companies might have become too large. The officers of Standard Oil felt that the only way they could make a profit and stay in business was to control everything large and small that might be of danger to it.

The meetings continued and might have gone on for two more years had Ida not had another of those unexpected surprises. She knew that smaller oil companies had been complaining for some thirty years that their oil tank cars were put on side tracks, their shipments delayed, and that the buyers of their oil were often threatened with harm if they did not cancel orders. Also it was said that railroad clerks reported their shipments from all the smaller companies to Standard Oil.

Everywhere Ida went she heard these complaints. Small businessmen told her that "the trust knows where we send every barrel of oil. Half our shipments never reach our customers." Ida did not believe this until she unexpectedly had the proof, thanks to a young man working at Standard Oil. His job was to burn piles of office records.

One afternoon as he was tossing papers into a furnace, he just happened to see the name of a friend who had once been his Sunday school teacher. He was an independent small oil refiner who was not part of the Standard Oil trust. The young man saw that the name appeared on many forms and he took the trouble to study the records. He discovered that the trust was receiving full information about every shipment his friend was making. Furthermore, the records showed that in every case Standard Oil representatives were instructed to "stop that shipment—get that trade." ✳

The young man could not sleep nights worrying about what was being done to his friend. Finally he took the set of records to his friend. The oil refiner was astonished at what he read. He knew all about Ida Tarbell from having read her articles and he immediately took the papers to her. That night they decided to print the documents but replace the real names with fictitious ones.

A few days after the article and the documents appeared in *McClure's*, Ida went to see Mr. Rogers in his office. He was furious and white with rage. Pointing to a copy of *McClure's* on his desk, he demanded to know where she got that "stuff."

Ida refused to disclose her source but informed Rogers that she now knew how they illegally obtained information regularly from the railroads about all shipments made by Standard Oil's competitors. After Rogers made a few more angry comments, Ida left his office. It was her last visit.

Each month the readers of *McClure's* eagerly awaited their copies of the magazine. They wondered what new evidence of dishonesty and greed Ida Tarbell would reveal. Over the years she showed them how powerful Standard Oil Company had become. It controlled banks, railroads, state legislatures, and even some United States senators. John D. Rockefeller was painted as a cruel and greedy man.

As for Standard Oil Company, it said nothing about the articles. Its head would not comment. "Not a word," Rockefeller said, "not a word about that misguided woman."

In the fall of 1904 two fat volumes of *The History of the Standard Oil Company* were published. The *New York Times* book reviewer wrote that "it is to the present time the most remarkable book of its kind ever written in this country." Most newspapers praised it highly, but a few disagreed. One magazine, *The Nation*, overlooked all the facts Ida had brought out, and said she was a hatemonger.

It was true that she heartily disliked John D. Rockefeller, so much so that she gladly did a special article at McClure's request. This was "John D. Rockefeller, A Character Study." In it she pointed out that although he was a poor youth, he had made himself a powerful man who became a bully. It was his greed, she said, that drove him to ruin hundreds if not thousands of honest men.

Ida wanted to be remembered as a historian, not a "muckraker." That was the name President Theodore Roosevelt gave to her, Baker, Steffens, and other writers who were revealing dishonesty in business and government. Of far greater importance, though, was what happened because of her history.

In 1906 the United States attorney general sued Standard Oil Company of New Jersey for not obeying the Sherman Anti-Trust Act. In 1907 a federal judge fined the company $29 million, and in 1911 the Supreme Court of the United States ordered the company to break apart its thirty-eight companies.

At last the trust was destroyed. The small oil producers and refiners finally had a chance to compete against the large companies. The American way of doing business fairly was restored. All this happened because of one woman, Ida Tarbell.

Chapter 11

A TRIP OUT WEST

If Ida thought that she was done with oil and the Standard Oil Company, she was mistaken. Oil was discovered in Kansas and Oklahoma in 1904, the year her book was published. The following spring McClure asked her to go out West and see what was happening. Mr. Tarbell had just died and Ida welcomed the trip to help her forget her father's death.

By the time she arrived in Kansas, hordes of people hoping to become wealthy had rushed there from all parts of the country. At the time every farmer in Kansas expected to strike oil on his land. Those who did found that a pipeline company suddenly appeared ready to connect their wells to its line. The Standard Oil people had arrived early to lay pipelines and take charge; on their own terms they quickly let it be known that they wanted no interference.

Earlier, when oil was discovered in Pennsylvania, the South Improvement Company had been able to buy up smaller companies and force most of those that would not join the trust out of business. This plan was not going to work again in Kansas. There the new Populist party represented the common people. It joined women's clubs and other political parties to fight Standard Oil.

"We'll take care of our own oil," they told the Standard Oil men as they introduced bills in the state legislature to control railroad and pipeline rates.

Ida spent ten days driving around southeastern Kansas and into Oklahoma where great wells were gushing. Everywhere people were trying to sell lots under which they swore there was oil. A few were selling stock in oil companies, many of which did not even exist. There was wild excitement and much dishonesty.

As Ida traveled around the state she discovered that many people had heard of her. A few who were friendly toward Standard Oil branded her a spy and an enemy of the people. Many small businessmen in the oil fields and some newspaper editors thought her a powerful friend in their fight against the giant Standard Oil.

She arrived in Tulsa, Oklahoma, late one night. Tulsa was a brand-new town with a few shabby buildings, dirt roads, and many strangers wandering about. It was a dangerous place for a single woman. Ida stayed at the only hotel, a small building hardly worthy of the name. There was no lock on her bedroom door so she moved the bureau against it, and slept on and off between listening for signs of possible danger.

Next morning as she was eating breakfast in the small dining room, the editor of the local newspaper came to her table. He wanted to know if she would go to his office for an interview. As soon as she finished eating, he led her to a large barnlike building next to the hotel where he took her into his office. They had just sat down when a young man came rushing in to tell Ida that she was in for a serenade.

"A serenade," she repeated. "What do you mean?"

He explained that some of the new settlers in Tulsa, who called themselves boomers, were making a tour of Oklahoma and their special train had just brought them back to town. They wanted to celebrate something, and when they learned that Ida Tarbell had arrived they decided to bring a band up to the hotel to welcome her.

"They want a speech," the youth said.

Ida had never given an unprepared speech and she begged her visitor to get her out of this.

"There's no escape," he told her. "It's too late." Then hearing a noise, he added, "They're here now!"

About forty members of the band, many of them Indians, crowded outside the building. Suddenly Ida had an idea.

"Go buy two boxes of the best cigars in Tulsa," she told the young man. She thrust a five-dollar bill into his hand. "Go quickly!"

By the time the band had finished the first piece, Ida was holding two open boxes of cigars. She stepped forward and handed cigars to all the band members and also to a group of Indians standing behind her.

She was tickled when she heard one of the Indians say to

his companion, "He all right." Later, as she walked about Tulsa, she saw men who had proudly tied her cigars to their shirt buttonholes with red ribbon. When they saw Ida, they smiled, nodded, and pointed to the cigars.

That afternoon the boomers and their friends insisted Ida lead a parade and ride in a large four-wheeled carriage, the only one in town. Ida's carriage headed the procession, the band followed, and behind it a large crowd of men and women marched in step to the music. A day or two later Ida left Tulsa loaded down with candy, magazines, books, and flowers, all given by grateful citizens.

Next she went to the capital of Kansas to call on Governor E.W. Hoch. She had heard that the legislature had passed laws intended to make Standard Oil the servant of the state. She asked the governor whether or not the laws would work. He told her he expected they would because people were determined to see that they did.

The next day she was asked to speak to a large group of businessmen and legislators and tell them what to do next. They were new to the oil business and to Standard Oil's operating methods.

She told them that the laws alone would not make them successful but that they had to learn to be as efficient and smart as their principal competitor, Standard Oil. Some of the men in the audience accused her of having joined Standard Oil. They had hoped to hear a rousing speech against

94

the oil trust. Others, though, agreed with her and admitted that they had much to learn if they were going to compete with Standard Oil.

Fortunately the wild Kansas oil boom and the laws that sought to control the oil trust encouraged other states to pass similar legislation. Congress also noticed what was going on in the West, as did President Theodore Roosevelt. He attacked big business and put an end to one large trust.

Congress then passed a law that created the Commerce and Labor Department with a Bureau of Corporations. President Roosevelt ordered the bureau to investigate the petroleum industry. It was 1906, the beginning of the end for the Standard Oil trust.

That year was also the beginning of the end for *McClure's*. Although Sam McClure was a sick man, he dreamed of expanding his business. Without telling his partners he organized a corporation that would operate a bank, sell life insurance, publish school books, and build inexpensive houses for poor people. All this, he reasoned, would help *McClure's* grow larger and more prosperous.

By the time McClure explained this to Ida he had convinced himself that it was a brilliant plan and must not be questioned. Ida told him bluntly that she would have no part of his project. As for John Phillips, he firmly refused to go along with the idea and spent the next six months trying to dissuade McClure from his impractical scheme. Since the two men could not agree, McClure bought out Phillips's interest in the business. At that point Ida resigned, as did Ray Stannard Baker, Lincoln Steffens, John Siddall, and other members of the staff.

Shortly thereafter Ida and John Phillips learned that the old *Frank Leslie's Illustrated Monthly* had just changed its name to *The American Magazine* and was looking for a buyer. Ida and the men who left *McClure's* used their savings to buy the magazine. In October, 1906 the first issue appeared and the search began for a series of articles that would attract new subscribers.

Immediately the staff turned to Ida. She had helped build *McClure's* with the series on Napoleon, Lincoln, and Standard Oil. What should it be this time? they wondered. Someone suggested they write about the tariff, the most important topic then being discussed in Washington and throughout the country.

The next day she was working on her outline.

Chapter 12

BOTH SIDES OF THE COIN

Before she left *The Chautauquan* to go to Paris in 1891, Ida believed that three wrongs were responsible for the repeated economic depressions in the country. The first was the unfair railroad rates and rebates given certain shippers. The second was the tariff, and the third was private ownership of natural resources such as lumber, oil, coal, iron ore, and other minerals. She had exposed the railroad rates in her Standard Oil book; now she would tackle the second wrong, the tariffs. Maybe some day, after she finished with tariffs, she would write about the third.

All she knew about the subject when she started her research was that a tariff is a list of "duties" or taxes charged on goods brought into a country. From the time our nation was founded, tariffs have been imposed on various imported articles. The very first bill passed in 1789 by the American Congress established the tariff. These taxes made imported goods more expensive to sell in the United States. Thus the struggling factories in New England could sell their products at lower prices than foreign-made goods.

Following the Civil War, duties on foods such as tea, coffee, and molasses were reduced but the high tariffs that protected American industries remained in effect. The problem has always been that each industry works to keep out foreign goods that would harm it. By 1900 the tariff was crowded with a variety of duties. Many of them were actually hurting the average American.

Few people understood tariffs or worried about their effects. However, by the time Ida began studying the subject, newspapers were carrying more and more articles about tariffs. Many Americans believed that the duties on iron, tin, beef, and sugar protected large corporations such as United States Steel, Armour, and the Havemeyer's sugar refineries. The duties permitted these and other corporations to overcharge the public because there was no competition from overseas.

Ida tackled the job with enthusiasm and her usual thoroughness. She went to Washington to read and study everything she could find relating to tariffs. Then she traveled about the country interviewing ex-congressmen who had worked on tariff bills. She was trying to discover their real reasons for backing one tariff or another.

What she found was that most congressmen had no personal interest in tariffs. They had allowed the lobbyists who represented big corporations to tell them how to vote. A lobbyist's job is to do everything possible to persuade legislators to vote a certain way. Thus these congressmen had accepted money and other favors from the lobbyists and voted as they were instructed. In addition, tariffs had become so complicated that few congressmen understood what they were voting for.

One man Ida interviewed was Joseph Wharton, a powerful executive in the iron and steel industry. He informed her that he controlled certain congressmen who voted as he told them to. He explained that it was not Congress that decided what the tariffs should be but the companies that would profit from them.

"I wrote the tariff bill of 1870," he boasted to Ida.

The Tarbell articles appeared off and on in *The American Magazine* for almost five years as she reviewed the history of tariffs and explained what they did. Then she aroused her readers with an article, "Where Every Penny Counts," in which she told what tariffs mean to the pocketbook of the average American. She showed how much the duties were really costing people when they bought items like shoes, thread, or wool.

She wrote: "The last man to be heard from at tariff hearings in this country is the man who buys the goods. . . at a time when wealth is rolling up as never before. . . a vast number of hard-working people in this country are really having a more difficult time making ends meet than they have ever had before."

She went on to lash out at big corporations that made millions because of the protective tariffs they enjoyed. Her articles did not go unnoticed. In 1909 Congress again was considering a tariff bill that would reduce some unfair duties. Thanks partly to Ida's articles, the House of Representatives removed or reduced a number of duties. However, when the bill reached the Senate, Senator Nelson W. Aldrich of Rhode Island succeeded in rewriting the bill so that it not only restored the duties that the House had removed, but increased some, especially on textiles.

The public was outraged but unable to do anything about it. Ida, in true muckraking style, went after Senator Aldrich. She visited many textile factories in Providence, Pawtucket, and Woonsocket, Rhode Island. There she found squalid working conditions that caused widespread disease and misery among the workers.

The article about the textile workers was illustrated with pictures of men and women who labored ten hours a day or more, along with photographs of the huge mansions built by Senator Aldrich and the mill owners. "This, then, is high protection's most perfect work," Ida wrote. "A state of half a million people turning out an annual product worth $187,000,000, the laborers in the chief industry underpaid, unstable and bent with disease, the average employers rich, self-satisfied, and as indifferent to social obligations as so many robber barons."

This ended her tariff series as well as further work on tariffs. She was exhausted, and realized the lobbyists were too strong for her to fight. Leaders of industry wanted protection from foreign competition and powerful labor unions backed them to protect their jobs. Little wonder Ida lost interest in the subject. Later, in 1916, President Woodrow Wilson asked her to serve on the new U.S. Tariff Commission, but she declined. She knew it would be a waste of time as long as the lobbyists controlled Congress.

Once she finished writing about tariffs Ida thought back to how she had criticized businessmen and pictured the worst conditions she could find in mills and factories. Suddenly she felt guilty. She had always thought of herself as a reporter and if that were true, should she not report the good as well as the bad? Many industrial leaders were trying to improve conditions for their workers. Shouldn't she tell the public about them, too?

She talked with Phillips and other staff members, who liked her idea and told her to go to work on it.

During the next four years Ida spent most of her time visiting laundries, steel mills, tanneries, mines, and factories. As she traveled and talked with workers she found that in every trade there were people who enjoyed their work. After visiting a mine she asked some miners why they stayed there.

"I like it," one answered. "I was brought up to it," another explained. "Nice and quiet in the mines," a third said.

"But it is so dangerous!" Ida protested.

"No worse than railroading," a stubby miner said, while his friend added, "My brother got killed by a horse last week."

Thomas Lynch, president of Frick Coke Company, told her about the improvements he had made in his mines. He invented the slogan "Safety first" because he believed in preventing accidents. Lynch also thought that good workers deserved good homes and the company provided seven thousand of them.

Ida spent ten days at the Ford Motor Company factory, talking with Henry Ford, other officials, and employees. Most places she visited impressed her favorably and her articles told of companies where labor and management cooperated and where working conditions were good.

Most readers did not expect Ida to praise big business and she became aware of this. She wrote that people were pleased when she described how workers were chopped up by big machines. However, when she told about companies that tried to avoid unnecessary accidents, subscribers complained that she had sold her soul to the corporations.

The series of articles concluded as Crowell Publishing took control of *The American Magazine*. Ida, Phillips, and others left because they were no longer partners, just employees. Ida went to her country home in Redding Ridge, Connecticut, which she had purchased a few years earlier. There she could be alone to think about her future. For the first time since leaving Titusville to join *McClure's*, she was without a steady income. She was free, but what should she do with her freedom and how would she earn a living?

Another surprise came along. This time it was Louis Alber of the Colt Alber Lecture Bureau. He signed her to work for seven weeks, to give forty-nine lectures in forty-nine places!

In 1935, Ida Tarbell, aware now that she had Parkinson's disease, began work on her autobiography.

Chapter 13

THE TWILIGHT YEARS

Oddly enough, the lecture tour Mr. Alber had arranged was for one of the chautauqua circuits. Some time after Ida had worked at *The Chautauquan* the owners decided to send culture into every small city and town. They hired lecturers, musicians, and entertainers to go on chautauqua circuits to present entertainment and serious programs. In each town the arrival of one of these groups was hailed as "Chautauqua Day."

Ida worried that she might not be able to make her audiences hear what she had to say. (This was before the time of microphones and loudspeakers.) She had heard something about "placing the voice" and went to a voice school. By the time the tour started in July she knew how to use her voice, but wondered whether she would be able to speak effectively once she was on the platform. She was instructed to give the same speech every afternoon.

There were seven in her circuit group and they performed in a khaki tent bound in red with a large khaki fence about it. Five young people sang for three quarters of an hour before Ida's lecture and again in the evening before the other speaker began. Ida enjoyed traveling with her companions as they worked, ate together, and lugged their suitcases to and from trains.

Each day Ida spoke about the hopeful and good things that were happening in America's industry. She soon found that most of her audiences had little interest in her subject. What they wanted her to speak about was the great European war that had started in 1914. Her agreement with Chautauqua was for a different kind of speech and she had to give the people what they did not want to hear.

Nevertheless she signed up for another tour because the pay was good and she needed the money. It was an exhausting routine. Most nights she would climb onto a train and try to get some rest in the sleeping car. There were missed train connections, changed train schedules, beds too hard or too soft, drafts, noises, and bad food. In the summer it would often be so hot she would push the bed over to the window to get a little air, but street noises often made sleep impossible.

In 1915 Henry Ford invited Ida to join him and a hundred other well-known Americans to sail to Europe on his "Peace Ship." It was his plan to get leaders of the warring nations together and work out a peaceful settlement. "We'll have the boys out of the trenches by Christmas," he promised. Ida declined. She felt it was a foolish idea that would never work. She was proven correct.

She was on her fourth speaking tour when the United States and Germany went to war. A few days later she was speaking at a large dinner in Cleveland. Just before she finished, a waiter handed her a telegram signed by President Woodrow Wilson. She ended her talk and then opened the telegram to read that the president had appointed her to the Women's Committee of the Council of National Defense. She wired her acceptance and two weeks later Dr. Anna H. Shaw, head of the committee, summoned her to Washington.

Ida went directly to a building on Pennsylvania Avenue where she found the other committee members standing in a dark dreary room. The only furniture was an old table and a few chairs, not enough for all the women. Ida saw that someone had to do something so she strode into the next office and dragged two chairs back to the room. Then someone helped her get more chairs from another office and they were able to start the meeting. Later she jokingly said that this was her best contribution to the war effort.

Ida had barely started work on the committee when she learned of her mother's death. She went to Titusville, arranged for the service, and stayed long enough to sell the house and the few things that were left. On her return to Washington she became ill and spent the next three months in the hospital, being treated for tuberculosis. When she was discharged she went to Dr. Harlow Brooks, her own doctor, to complain about her trembling, her weak right leg, and her stiff tongue. Dr. Brooks discovered that she had Parkinson's disease. He knew that the shaking and muscle weakness would spread slowly from her right side to the left. There was no cure for it.

"Don't worry about it," he told her. "Go on about your life." He did not want her to know what was wrong. She returned to her work on the war committee that was busy giving helpful advice and information about living in wartime.

Meanwhile Ida's old friend John Phillips had become editor of *The Red Cross Magazine*. Once the war ended he asked Ida to go to France to report on that war-torn country. At the same time President Wilson appointed her an official observer at the Paris Peace Conference.

Ida sailed from New York, her trunk filled with gifts for Madame Marillier and Charles Seignobos, who had also been a friend in Paris. Into the trunk she had stuffed blankets, stockings, high-laced boots, woolen tights, and other clothing. In addition she carried on board the largest ham she could find, thinking her friends would need food.

The ship landed at Bordeaux and Ida arranged for the trunk to be shipped to Paris. Then she carried her suitcase and the enormous ham from the dock to the train. She managed to find a seat and with difficulty stored the ham on an overhead rack. The first time the train sped around a curve the ham rolled off and fell, nearly killing two Quakers sitting beneath it. After that Ida held it in her lap. When she reached Paris she delivered the ham and the contents of the trunk to her grateful friends.

Bombs had changed the Paris she had known and loved. Many buildings had been damaged and there was little in the stores for people to buy. She was greatly cheered, however, by a reunion with August Jaccaci, Lincoln Steffens, William Allen White, and Ray Stannard Baker, who were there to report on the Peace Conference.

Soon after the conference ended and Ida had returned to the United States, she resumed her lecture tours. She found this more difficult than before the war. For one thing, most of the audiences had not heard of her and she was strange to them. For another, her schedule was busier and she frequently found it necessary to wait for late trains, sit up all night, and go without meals. She put up with the discomforts because at the end of the tour she would return to her Redding Ridge home, where she could putter about in her garden. She had become increasingly fond of the place and the opportunity it gave her to be alone.

In 1924 her brother Will, who had lost all his money and was in debt, became quite ill. Rather than put him in a sanitarium, Ida took him and his wife into her home. This ended her privacy and the great pleasure she had from her country home. Now she needed more income to support two extra people.

She had talked with Sam McClure about doing a third volume of the Standard Oil history and letting him use the material for another series in his magazine. Then Judge

Elbert H. Gary, chairman of the United States Steel Corporation, called her to urge that she write his biography.

Gary, a lawyer, had become a county judge, and later had organized United States Steel. He founded Gary, Indiana, a steel town, believed in paying high wages to his employees and providing safety measures to protect them. However, he was opposed to all unions and required that his workers put in long hours every day.

Ida did not like the man, but she needed money to pay Will's debts and to support the three of them. Ten thousand dollars for the book and ten thousand dollars for the serial articles in *McClure's* were well worth earning. In writing about Gary she had to overlook much that she did not approve of, but she managed to do a thorough job just the same. Later she was criticized by some for praising a steel man who, it was said, was no better than the Standard Oil people.

McCall's magazine had asked Ida to visit Florida and write about the 1925 land boom there. The following year the editor sent her to Italy to write a series of articles telling what it was like to live under the dictator Benito Mussolini.

Back in the United States she continued her lecture work part of each year until 1932, when she no longer had enough strength for speaking and constant travel. That year she published a biography of Owen D. Young, chairman of the board of General Electric Company. Three years later she agreed to write her life story for Macmillan and *All in the Day's Work* appeared in 1939.

By now her hands shook so hard that she had to sit on them to keep them quiet. She found herself pitching forward and her legs jerked her along unsteadily.

"Surely," she told Dr. Brooks, "this is not just old age." He shook his head gravely and confessed that she had indeed had Parkinson's disease for several years. "But you'll live a hundred years," he assured her. She wondered how she could support herself regardless of how long she lived. Soon she was forced to sell forty of her lovely acres in Redding Ridge, leaving ten acres.

What she never knew was that certain friends saw to it that she had an income without her ever knowing its source. She continued to grow more and more feeble. Her brother Will died and her sister Sarah came to live with her. She refused to give up, received visitors, and worked every day on another book, *Life After Eighty*, but never finished it.

One day, just before Christmas, 1943, Sarah could not wake her. Attendants from the Bridgeport Hospital lifted her gently onto a stretcher and carried her to their ambulance. She lay in her hospital bed quietly for several days without awakening. Then on January 6, 1944, the lively but always gracious woman, who dared to stand up to the mighty Standard Oil Company and reveal its ugly secrets, died quietly.

111

Ida Minerva Tarbell 1857-1944

1857 Ida Minerva Tarbell is born on November 5 in Erie County, Pennsylvania. James Buchanan is inaugurated president. Supreme Court issues the Dred Scott decision, strengthening the cause of slavery. *The Atlantic Monthly* is founded. The New York *Daily Times* becomes the *New York Times*.

1858 Abrahma Lincoln and Stephen Douglas debate over the slavery issue. U.S. and China sign peace and trade treaty.

1859 Abolitionist John Brown is hanged for leading raid in Harper's Ferry, Virginia. Suez Canal construction begins. First oil well is drilled at Titusville, Pennsylvania. Charles Darwin publishes *On the Origin of Species by Natural Selection.*

1860 Tarbell family moves to Rouseville, Pennsylvania. Abraham Lincoln is elected president; South Carolina secedes from the Union in protest. British Food and Drug Act is passed.

1861 Ten southern states secede, forming the Confederate States of America and electing Jefferson Davis their president. Confederate attack on Fort Sumter begins the Civil War; Confederates win first battle of Bull Run. Russia declares freedom for serfs.

1862 Robert E. Lee heads Confederate army; Civil War battles are fought at Antietam, Fredericksburg, and Chattanooga; *Monitor* and *Merrimac* engage in first ironclad sea battle. Otto von Bismarck becomes prime minister of Prussia. Mark Twain becomes a reporter for the Nevada newspaper *Territorial Enterprise.*

1863 Emancipation Proclamation: Abraham Lincoln declares all slaves free. Lincoln delivers the Gettysburg Address. French occupy Mexico City; Archduke Maximillian is declared emperor of Mexico.

1864 Abraham Lincoln is reelected president. Ulysses S. Grant becomes commander-in-chief of Union army. Union General William Sherman begins his march through Georgia to the sea; Savannah, Georgia, surrenders to Union army.

1865 President Abraham Lincoln is assassinated; Andrew Johnson becomes president. Confederate General Robert E. Lee surrenders to Union General Ulysses S. Grant at Appomattox Court House, Virginia; Civil War ends. Thirteenth Amendment to the Constitution abolishes slavery. Union stockyards open in Chicago. *San Francisco Examiner* and *San Francisco Chronicle* are founded.

1866 Fourteenth Amendment outlaws voting discrimination. London Stock Exchange crashes on "Black Friday." Transatlantic telegraph cable is completed. Prussia and Italy form an alliance against Austria.

1867 U.S. buys Alaska from Russia for $7,200,000. Reconstruction Acts are passed. French troops leave Mexico; Emperor Maximillian is executed.

1868 President Andrew Johnson is impeached, but later acquitted. Ulysses S. Grant is elected president. Benjamin Disraeli becomes British prime minister; resigns later this year. P.D. Armour's meat-packing plant opens in Chicago.

1869 U.S. National Prohibition party is formed in Chicago. First U.S. transcontinental railroad is completed. Suez Canal opens.

1870 Tarbell family moves to Titusville, Pennsylvania. John D. Rockefeller founds the Standard Oil Company. Rome is annexed to Italy and becomes its capital. France declares war on Prussia; Napoleon III surrenders at Battle of Sedan.

1871 Chicago is devastated by the Great Chicago Fire. Labor unions are legalized in Britain. German Empire is established, with William I as emperor. Henry Stanley finds lost explorer

David Livingstone near Lake Tanganyika in Africa.

1872 Ulysses S. Grant is reelected president, defeating editor and reformer Horace Greeley. Congressional committee probes Standard Oil Company. Confederates are pardoned in General Amnesty Act.

1873 Congress establishes gold as the U.S. monetary standard. Spain is proclaimed a republic.

1874 Indo-China becomes a French protectorate. Alfonso XII becomes king of Spain. Chicago *Daily Tribune* is taken over by Joseph Medill. Society for the Prevention of Cruelty to Children is founded in New York.

1875 "Whiskey Ring" revenue officials are indicted for conspiracy to defraud the government of whiskey revenues. Civil Rights Act is passed, but Supreme Court declares it invalid in 1883.

1876 Ida Tarbell enters Allegheny College. Winner of presidential election is in dispute. Congressional committee again examines Standard Oil. Sitting Bull massacres General Custer's troops at Little Big Horn. Secretary of War William Belknap is impeached for taking bribes for the sale of trading posts in Indian Territory. Alexander Graham Bell patents the telephone.

1877 Presidential electoral commission rules that Rutherford B. Hayes won the 1876 elections. Russia and Serbia declare war on Turkey; Russia invades Rumania.

1878 Thomas Edison invents the incandescent electric lamp. Turkey and Russia sign armistice.

1879 Construction of Panama Canal begins. Zulus massacre British troops; Zulu chiefs sign peace agreement with British.

1880 Ida Tarbell becomes preceptress of Poland Union Seminary. James Garfield is elected president. Andrew Carnegie develops first large steel furnace.

1881 President Garfield is assassinated; Chester A. Arthur becomes president. France establishes freedom of the press. Tsar Alexander II of Russia is assassinated.

1882 Ida Tarbell leaves Poland Seminary. John D. Rockefeller organizes the Standard Oil Trust in Ohio. United Press syndicate is founded; folds in 1893; is refounded in 1907. U.S. bans Chinese immigration for next ten years.

1883 Ida Tarbell joins *The Chautauquan* staff. Northern Pacific Railroad line is completed. World's first skyscraper, ten stories high, is built in Chicago. New York's Brooklyn Bridge is opened.

1884 Grover Cleveland is elected president. Samuel McClure founds the McClure Newspaper Syndicate. France presents the Statue of Liberty to the United States.

1885 Civil War Union General Ulysses S. Grant dies. Louis Pasteur develops a rabies vaccine.

1886 Anarchists riot in Chicago's Haymarket Square. American Federation of Labor is founded. Andrew Carnegie publishes *Triumphant Democracy*.

1887 Interstate Commerce Commission, first U.S. regulatory commission, is established.

1888 Benjamin Harrison is elected president. Kaiser Wilhelm II becomes emperor of Germany.

1889 London dock workers go on strike. Austrian Crown Prince Archduke Rudolph commits suicide. Barnum and Bailey Circus opens in London.

1890 Ida Tarbell leaves *The Chautauquan*. Congress passes the Sherman Anti-Trust Act, although Presidents Cleveland and McKinley do not enforce it. A merger forms the American Tobacco Company. Japan holds its first general elections. Influenza epidemic sweeps the world.

1891 Ida Tarbell goes to Paris; receives first payment from Cincinnati *Times-Star*. Ohio judge dismantles Standard Oil Trust. The American Sugar Refining Company is formed by a merger. Famine hits Russia. Earthquake in Japan kills 10,000 people.

1892 Ida Tarbell publishes "France Adorée" in *Scribner's Magazine*. Grover Cleveland is elected president. Ohio courts rule that Standard Oil violates Ohio's antimonopoly laws; Standard Oil reincorporates in New Jersey.

1893 Financial and industrial depression, the Panic of 1893, sets off the Progressive Movement in the U.S., the background for the muckraking movement. Henry Ford constructs his first automobile.

1894 Ida Tarbell interviews Henry Drummond in Glasgow; begins the Napoleon series. National Municipal League is formed to oust corrupt political machines in city governments. Korea and Japan declare war on China.

1895 Ida Tarbell begins Lincoln research in Kentucky. Supreme Court rules that the Sherman Anti-Trust Act does not apply to manufacturing combinations. Cuba begins fighting Spain for independence. China is defeated in war with Japan. Turks massacre Armenians.

1896 Tarbell publishes *The Early Life of Abraham Lincoln*; enters Clifton Springs Sanatarium. William McKinley is elected president. Klondike Gold Rush begins in Alaska. Adolph S. Ochs takes over the *New York Times*; shows his intent toward serious journalism with the slogans "All the news that's fit to print" and "It will not soil your breakfast cloth."

1897 First U.S. subway line opens in Boston. Severe famine hits India.

1898 Tarbell beings work on Carl Schurz's biography. Spanish-American War begins; ends in Treaty of Paris; U.S. acquires Philippines, Puerto Rico, and Guam. U.S. annexes Hawaii. Cuba gains independence from Spain. Bubonic plague epidemic kills three million people in China and India over next ten years.

1899 Tarbell moves to New York City. Boer War begins in South Africa.

1900 Tarbell publishes *The Life of Abraham Lincoln*. William McKinley is reelected president. 231 civilians are killed in China's Boxer Rebellion.

1901 Tarbell meets Samuel McClure in Europe to discuss Standard Oil article. President William McKinley is assassinated; Theodore Roosevelt becomes president. J.P. Morgan starts U.S. Steel Corporation. England's Queen Victoria dies at 81 after reigning 64 years.

1902 Tarbell's Standard Oil series begins. President Roosevelt begins breaking up trusts and monopolies; dissolves a railroad monopoly in the northwest; becomes first president to force arbitration of a laborers' strike. Cuba becomes an independent republic. South Africa Boer War ends.

1903 Theodore Roosevelt wins presidential election. Muckraking emerges in January issue of *McClure's Magazine* with articles by Lincoln Steffens, Ray Stannard Baker, and Ida Tarbell. President Roosevelt has Congress establish the Bureau of Corporations to investigate corrupt business practices. Orville and Wilbur Wright fly the first airplane at Kitty Hawk, North Carolina.

1904 Macmillan publishes Tarbell's *History of the Standard Oil Company*. Thomas W. Lawson's article "Frenzied Finance" exposes corporate irresponsibility. Russia declares war on Japan.

1905 Franklin Sumner Tarbell (Ida's father) dies. Russo-Japanese war ends in Treaty of

Portsmouth. Russian troops massacre workers in St. Petersburg on "Bloody Sunday." Charles Edward Russell publishes his exposé *The Greatest Trust in the World*. Albert Einstein introduces his special theory of relativity.

1906 President Theodore Roosevelt introduces the term "muckrakers" in an April 14 speech. Edwin Markham exposes child labor in *Children in Bondage*. Upton Sinclair's *The Jungle* and Samuel Hopkins Adam's *Great American Fraud* help pass the Beef Inspection Act and the Pure Food and Drugs Act. Hepburn Act increases Interstate Commerce Commission's control over railroad fare hikes. David Graham Phillips's "The Treason of the Senate" helps pass the Seventeenth Amendment, calling for election of senators by popular vote. U.S. Attorney General sues Standard Oil of New Jersey for violating the Sherman Anti-Trust Act. Phillips Publishing company is formed to publish *American Magazine*; Tarbell and other writers buy the magazine.

1907 Charles Edward Russell publishes *The Uprising of the Many*, exposing U.S. efforts to extend democracy to other countries. Brand Whitlock publishes *The Turn of the Balance*, an anti-capital punishment novel. *American Magazine* publishes "He Knew Lincoln." A federal judge fines Standard Oil $29 million. J.P. Morgan imports $1 million in gold to stop the "Panic of 1907" run on banks. Roosevelt bars Japanese immigration.

1908 William Howard Taft is elected president. Ford Motor Company manufactures the first Model "T" car. General Motors Corporation is formed.

1909 Explorer Robert E. Peary reaches the North Pole. Motion picture newsreels first appear in theaters.

1910 Japan annexes Korea. China abolishes slavery.

1911 Supreme Court supports Roosevelt's breaking of oil and tobacco monopolies, reversing its 1895 pro-trust decision. Standard Oil Company is dissolved into several companies. Chinese Revolution begins; Manchu dynasty falls; Chinese Republic is proclaimed, with Sun Yat-sen as president.

1912 Woodrow Wilson is elected president. Muckraking movement is effectively dead. Columbia University School of Journalism is set up by Joseph Pulitzer bequest. The *Titanic* collides with an iceberg and sinks on its first voyage.

1913 Balkan Wars begin. Mahatma Gandhi is arrested in India for leading passive resistance movement. Industrialist J.P. Morgan dies. John D. Rockefeller founds the Rockefeller Institute with $100 million grant.

1914 Federal Trade Commission is set up to regulate businesses engaged in interstate commerce. Garrilo Princip assassinates Archduke Francis Ferdinand in Sarajevo; World War I Begins. Panama Canal opens.

1915 Tarbell becomes independent free-lance writer; begins lecturing. World War I continues: Germans sink the *Lusitania*. Einstein introduces his general theory of relativity.

1916 Woodrow Wilson is reelected president. World War I continues; Allies begin offensive in Macedonia. Arabs revolt against Turks.

1917 U.S. declares war on Germany and enters World War I. Tsar Nicholas II of Russia abdicates; Bolshevik revolution begins in St. Petersburg. Upton Sinclair publishes *King Coal*.

1918 World War I ends. Austria, Hungary, Bavaria, and Germany become republics. Czechoslovakia and Yugoslavia declare independence.

1919 *Red Cross Magazine* sends Tarbell to Paris for armistice and Versailles Conference.
   Eighteenth Amendment prohibits sale of alcoholic beverages. First League of Nations meeting
   is held in Paris. Benito Mussolini forms fascist party in Italy.

1920 Tarbell resumes lecturing. Warren G. Harding is elected president. U.S. passes Nineteenth
   Amendment, giving women the right to vote.

1921 U.S. signs peace treaties with Germany and Austria. Paris conference of Allies sets German
   war debts at $33 billion. India's Mahatma Gandhi launches civil disobedience campaign.

1922 Union of Soviet Socialist Republics is formed. Fascists march on Rome; Mussolini gains
   dictatorial powers in Italy. Gandhi is imprisoned for civil disobedience in India.

1923 Tarbell publishes *In the Footsteps of the Lincolns*. President Warren G. Harding dies; Calvin
   Coolidge becomes president. Nazi Party leader Adolph Hitler is imprisoned for unsuccessful
   coup attempt, the "Beer Hall Putsch."

1924 Calvin Coolidge wins presidential election. Soviet power struggle follows Nikolai Lenin's death.
   William Randolph Hearst founds the tabloid *Daily Mirror*. New York *Herald Tribune* is
   created from merger of New York *Tribune* and *Weekly Tribune*.

1925 Schoolteacher John Scopes is convicted for teaching the theory of evolution, but is later
   acquitted. Reza Kahn becomes Shah of Iran; establishes Pahlavi dynasty.

1926 Tarbell interviews Benito Mussolini for *McCall's Magazine*. Robert H. Goddard develops first
   liquid-fuel rocket. General workers' strike is called in England.

1927 Charles A. Lindbergh makes first solo transatlantic airplane flight. Trotsky is expelled from
   Soviet Communist Party; Joseph Stalin takes power. Upton Sinclair publishes *Oil!*

1928 Herbert Hoover is elected president. Congress approves $32 million to enforce Prohibition.
   Stalin institutes Five Year Plan for industry and collective farms in U.S.S.R.

1929 U.S. stock market crashes, causing depression, unemployment, and worldwide economic crisis.
   In Chicago's St. Valentine's Day Massacre, members of the Moran gang are shot by rival
   mobsters. Arabs attack Palestinian Jews in dispute over Wailing Wall.

1930 More than 1,300 U.S. banks close due to stock market crash. Hitler's Nazi party gains a
   majority in German elections. Ras Tafari is crowned emperor Haile Selassie I of Ethiopia.

1931 Gangster Al Capone is imprisoned for income tax evasion. Wiley Post and Harold Gatty are
   first to fly around the world. All German banks close following bankruptcy of Databank.
   Lincoln Steffens publishes his autobiography.

1932 Franklin D. Roosevelt wins landslide presidential victory. Famine sweeps U.S.S.R.

1933 *McClure's Magazine* folds. Twenty-first Amendment repeals Prohibition. Adolph Hitler
   becomes German chancellor; democratic Weimar Republic falls; Hitler names Goebbels
   Minister of Propaganda. Nazis construct first concentration camp for Jews; all German
   political parties except Nazi are banned. Fulgencio Batista leads a *coup d'etat* in Cuba.

1934 Hitler becomes president of Germany. U.S.S.R. joins League of Nations. FBI agents shoot
   "Public Enemy Number One" John Dillinger.

1935 Tarbell begins her autobiography. Persia changes its name to Iran. Germany passes anti-
   Jewish Nuremberg laws. Chiang Kai-chek becomes president of Chinese executive.

1936 Franklin D. Roosevelt is reelected president. Mussolini and Hitler form Rome-Berlin Axis.
   King Edward VIII abdicates the throne of England. China's Chiang Kai-shek declares war on

Japan. Trotsky is exiled from Russia. Spanish Civil War begins.

1937 George VI is crowned king of England. Japan seizes Peking, Tientsin, and Shanghai. John D. Rockefeller dies.

1938 House Committee on Un-American Activities convenes. Germans invade and annex Austria.

1939 Macmillan publishes Tarbell's autobiography, *All in the Day's Work*. World War II begins; Germany invades Poland; England and France declare war on Germany. Spanish Civil War ends; England and France recognize Franco's government.

1940 Franklin D. Roosevelt is reelected president for a third term. Winston Churchill becomes prime minister of Great Britain. World War II continues: Germany invades Norway, Denmark, Holland, Belgium, and Luxembourg; German troops occupy Paris; Italy declares war on England and France; Germany bombs London.

1941 Will Tarbell (Ida's brother) dies. World War II continues: Hitler invades Russia; Japan bombs Pearl Harbor; U.S. and Britain declare war on Japan; Germany and Italy declare war on U.S.; U.S. declares war on Germany and Italy.

1942 World War II continues: Japan captures Manila and Singapore; U.S. troops land in Solomon Islands and North Africa; Battles of El Alamein (Egypt) and Solomon Islands.

1943 Tarbell goes into a coma. World War II continues: German forces in Stalingrad surrender; Italian government collapses; Allies land in Italy; fighting in North Africa ceases.

1944 Ida Tarbell dies on January 6 in Bridgeport, Connecticut. Allied forces invade Normandy and enter Paris; U.S. invades the Philippines; Battle of the Bulge begins.

INDEX- *Page numbers in boldface type indicate illustrations.*

118

119

ABOUT THE AUTHOR

Adrian Paradis's writing career started with a dream—a book for boys on how to earn money. He wrote and sold it and since then has written almost fifty books for young people on a wide variety of subjects, principally careers. He has been a hotel manager, librarian, corporate executive, head of a commission, Vermont planning and now editor of a small publishing company specializing in New England town histories. He and his wife live in Sugar Hill, New Hampshire.

120